NOVEMBER   1948

Drawings by Arthur Balderacchi

———————————

University Press of Virginia

Charlottesville and London

NOVEMBER   1948

1

"That's the effect of living backwards,"
the Queen said kindly: "it always makes
one a little giddy at first—"

"Living backwards!" Alice repeated
in great astonishment. "I never heard
of such a thing!"

"—but there's one great advantage in it,
that one's memory works both ways."

Through the Looking Glass

Rock Island seemed to be the name of town after town. How could they tell them apart? As I looked out of the window of the Pullman car, sliding through woods that were brown and bony white in the morning sunshine, I wondered how many miles there could be to travel, how many people, how

1

many towns so far from England. Who could find their way here? Ohio and Illinois. Odd names on an unfamiliar map, blurs or long vistas through the pitted glass next to my pillow. In the berth above, Mother was crying softly, unhappy or in pain. No one else seemed to be awake. No one to hear. No one to see the rise and fall of telegraph wires cutting the landscape with the rhythm of the train. Later in Chicago, we would board the new train called the Golden State. Hollywood and Los Angeles, deserts and cowboys, the West of boyhood movies. Mark Twain dying with the return of Halley's comet. Dust and death in the sunset.

I remembered other journeys in a distant world. Once when we went hiking in the Pennines, my father had asked the train driver to stop between stations, so that we could jump out in the dawn light and begin our long ascent, the flat-topped shapes of Whernside and Ingleborough looming but not yet visible where we expected them on the horizon, light drops of mist falling in the grayness. Then returning home in the warm, smoky carriage, lying in the strings of the luggage rack, above flushed and noisy men singing "Danny Boy" and "Loch Lomond." Afterwards, with our friend Dave

2

walking beside us, I atop my father's shoulders, we climbed up the steep, tree-lined alley from Apperley Bridge, and I knew that without my father I would be running from specters, from the moving shadows lurking behind trees, now powerless to hurt me. That was two years and nine months before; I was seven.

A more recent journey: we had said goodbye to Dave and his wife at their tiny house in northern London and taken two cabs to Victoria Station. My father was late, and I felt certain this time that we would miss the boat train and miss the boat as well. I lived again the time in Leeds when he told my brother and me to wait for him in front of the bus station and returned an hour and a half later to find us rainsoaked and crying, ready to beg strangers for help. Now we stood, my sister, brother, mother, and I, on the platform of that gloomy, cavernous station, the noise of entering and leaving trains clashing with loudspeakers and cab brakes squealing and the tack-tack-tack of high-heeled shoes along the pavement. It was four-thirty and already dark outside. The train would leave in five minutes. At last a porter rushed up with another load of suitcases and the second trunk, which was stowed in the luggage car.

My father strode leisurely across to us, smiling as if to say that the train would have waited.

We were off. A chug, a whistle from the distant engine, a small hesitation, and soon the clickety snaking race out of the city. As we sped through the downs and into the tunnels toward Southampton, I stood by myself in the corridor, ignoring the warnings about putting my head out of the window, and watched the rush of night and lights and passing trains. My hand smelled of the brass fittings and handrail. I was crying, but crying with pleasure, singing what I had heard Gracie Fields sing on the wireless: "Soon I'll be sailing, far across the sea. . . . Oh please remember me." When the train slowed into Southampton, rattling through the docks, the great red funnels of the *Queen Elizabeth* lifted up then disappeared behind the black buildings of the port.

In Chicago we had to change train stations to board the Golden State, and during the taxi ride I watched my father counting and recounting the money in his wallet. The Pullman car was, he had been told, the only available reserved accommodations on transcontinental trains, and half the money my parents had gathered together for the new country went to pay for the tickets. Our one breakfast on the New York Central train—eating proudly from thick, heavy silverware and watching dark-skinned waiters carry covered plates or pour coffee from high above the table—had cost twelve dollars, more my father said later than his budget for a whole day. He was worried about another two days of dining car prices. So when we arrived at La Salle Street Station, he walked away with my sister and came back with paper bags full of fruit and bread and cheese, which we ate most of the way across to Los Angeles.

I had always loved dining cars, even when we didn't eat in them—or when the train was still. At home we had sneaked into the empty carriages waiting on shunting tracks, taking our games and our pet white mice, which played on the tables and sometimes raced for us, leaving little turds behind them. But on the Southern Pacific we missed the dining car altogether, living on the snacks. Father said the porter with the dining bell lifted his nose when he walked by our compartment, but we were rarely there. We spent most of our time in the ob-

5

servation car and in the lounge, where the porter had become our friend. His name was Vergil Smock.

I asked Mr. Smock, as the train crossed the border into California, for another special Coke. He had told us that a cherry or lemon slice improved soft drinks, and when I realized that a Coke was a soft drink (wondering what made a hard one), I began to ask confidently for lemon Cokes. This time he said it was my turn to serve it. Since my brother and I had been helping him for two days, adding lemon or olives to the drinks he mixed and sometimes carrying them to other passengers, I knew how to prepare my Coke. I scooped a half glass of ice, no longer a novelty for me, siphoned in the soda and the deep brown syrup, and split a slice of lemon over the top of the glass. Then I sat, sipping my Coke, as the train clanked across the bridge and entered the last leg of our journey.

"Please tell me more about California, Mr. Smock." "Well, son, you can see for yourself," he said. "Just look around." He stood with one arm resting on the upholstered seat, his white jacket unblemished and stark against his black skin, and swept his other hand to draw the horizon. To me it appeared no different from Arizona and the other states we had been crossing, and I worried that, like Phoenix and Tucson, Los Angeles might be another faded blotch in the desert. Feeling already a little defrauded, I looked out of the tinted window at scrubby brush and more cactus and long waves of watery-looking plain that I had come to know as mirage. If I admitted that this place mocked my dreams of the past year, there was the consolation that we were still several hours away from Los Angeles.

"Where do you live, Mr. Smock?" He hesitated and said he didn't think I would be familiar with the name, but near to Pasadena, which was not far from where we were going. I knew that my mother had asked him to visit us in our new house and how he had smiled without answering. Now he told me how close we would be and how he would come to take my brother and me for a ride. My sister if she wanted, though maybe another time. He talked of football and baseball in a language new to me, telling me about Marion Motley and Jackie Robinson, and how he was a Dodgers fan. He would take us, he said, to see the route of the Rose Parade and where the Rose Bowl game would be played.

"I'll come and show you around after I get back next time from Chicago. Check?"

"Check," I said.

§

We were coming down out of dry and rocky mountains, twisting into Southern California. Already in the dusk I had seen some orange groves. Ahead were lights spread out like patterned stars, but there were no stars in the sky. In spite of the air-conditioning, the air seemed different, richer, more intense. I saw reflections of my own face in the mirroring windows of the observation car, round and smiling. A man next to me grunted something and turned, shoving me with his leg. He was grotesquely fat with a thick vein across his forehead, and I could see that, in the cool air, little drops of sweat were falling from the ends of his wiry gray hair.

"To this land," he said, lifting up his glass for a toast, "this land of the sundown sea."

The meaning of the words didn't register with me, but they sounded right. A sudden velvet darkness, with endless sprawling lights. Land of the sundown sea.

"Yes sireeh," said the man, and he leaned over as if to squash me. "Everything in Southern California is upside down. Just remember that. Or downside up. Got it?"

"Downside up," I said.

"You got it."

"Check."

𝔖

Stepping from a transcontinental train into Union Station was to enter a world of illumination, color, and noise. Unlike Victoria or Penn Station, this seemed intimate, with rows of soft seats and bright tiles decorating the walls. Whether I saw those faces familiar to me from Saturday matinees, or whether such people were here just part of a California breed, I thought I saw them. Beautiful, tall people, some with large dogs, guided with their luggage by uniformed black men, who seemed to know everything and to be able to carry, on their dollies, a dozen suit and hat cases. We waited for a few minutes until a man resembling my father,

9

though taller and with short, cropped hair, approached slowly.

"Are you Jerry? Lorna? I'm George. Mother's in the car; you know she doesn't meet people easily." He sounded as if he spoke through a hole in his chest, deep and soft.

After shaking hands with all of us and whispering "George" to each, he introduced another man, Uncle Bill, Auntie Madge's husband, who had kept a few feet away and who moved in now to help with our luggage.

"Howdoo," he said. "Mighty pleased."

June whispered, "Big Bill Campbell," and tried not to laugh. Big Bill introduced songs from the Old West on the BBC. I too had to look down to keep from giggling.

We left the lights of the station to step into soft night air. Palm trees grew near the station. Yellow taxis and other long cars purred like happy animals around the entrance, white headlights sweeping across walls and people, deep shadows behind. When we collected our steamer trunks—now just distressed copies of the ones my father had repaired and shellacked—we used Uncle George's small dolly and wheeled our belongings to the cars. Uncle

Bill and my father pushed one of the trunks into the rear, a second onto the roof of Bill's square-backed and wood-sided station wagon, which seemed to be aptly named.

We squeezed into the two cars, and I rode with Uncle George, who began to point out City Hall, Olvera Street, Broadway, and some of the other streets as we drove along. Then as I half listened and felt the gentle weight of long travel, I woke abruptly to a nightmare of sirens and spinning red lights. I made out a large van that I recognized as an ambulance, though bigger than any I had seen. Headlights coming our way were suddenly still, while we were limited to one lane, as if lining up to view a coffin. Figures dressed in white bent over one writhing body while policemen drew a sheet across another; brilliant patches of crimson grew upon the sheet in the blinding whiteness of the cars' headlights. A man with torn clothes sat heaving against the front tire of a car, surrounded by glittering diamond-shards of glass. He had thrown up on his shirt. My mother looked across, groaned, and turned away sobbing.

Uncle George began to speak with a louder voice.

"But this invites the occult mind,
Cancels our physics with a sneer,
And spatters all we knew of denouement
Across the expedient and wicked stones."

"Oh please, don't," my mother said. She sat on the other side of my new grandmother, whom I still hadn't clearly seen. When we got to the car, Grandma had stayed in the back seat, smiling quickly as the door opened and stepping out, though only long enough it seemed to touch the ground with her feet. She gave no one hugs except my father, and even his was abrupt. She spoke a little when she got back in the car, nodding or muttering when asked a question, but it was my uncle who did most of the talking. My mother said nothing. Grandma sat between my mother and myself, looking if anything gloomier than my mother. I could just make out a heavy-set woman, whose eyes appeared sunken in the dimness of the car, as dark as her skin, which was olive like my father's but coarser and looser. Her hair was gray and thick, pulled together near the top of her head. She didn't look out at the accident, and when my uncle said "You'll have to get used to it," my grandmother said:

"Some things you never get used to. George for one."

"I'll tell you what kind of lady this is," my uncle said, as he pointed his thumb over the seat in the direction of his mother. "When she goes down to the market or goes anywhere for that matter, she comes home with money in her purse, and I mean bills as well as change. That's because she stares at the ground. Don't you, Mother?"

"And what if I do?"

"I'm just saying. You may get used to her, Lorna, although it will take some doing. I'm not sure I've managed after thirty-six years."

"George," said the woman in the front seat, who became my Auntie Minnie. "You're talking about your own ma. Enough, for Godsake."

"Apologies," said George, "all round. And apologies for the accident, Lorna, though I guess in the car capital of America they're unavoidable. Not that there's really any such thing as an accident, if you think about it. How about you, Carl? Everything all right? I should have said to look down—like your grandma here. She saves herself trouble as well as money."

🐚

I slept that night in a trundle bed, placed at the back of my grandmother's long sewing room. The blanket smelled of mothballs. Across the years I can hear the terrific chirping of crickets piercing the soft night. Adults chirp their own language on the floor above. Muffled horns and sirens alternate on the boulevard down the hill. The *Queen Elizabeth* is the largest passenger ship in the world, displacing 83,000 tons. Her length allows her to span three of the biggest Atlantic waves. Built at Clydeside, in Scotland, she was used during the war to carry troops and had the speed to outrun the German U-boats. I see a man sobbing by a ravaged car, but my eye avoids the other figures, stained and frightening on the road. Elsewhere near a sundown sea the room rocks gently with the rhythm of trains. Rock Island, Pennsy, Santa Fe. Rock Island, Pennsy, Santa Fe.

🐚

After the darkness and rain of a Yorkshire autumn, Los Angeles shone that first morning like a new dream. We drank tea on the tiled balcony, watching the few cars and an occasional streetcar on the boulevard below. Like a broken eggshell, my mother said, the mountains stretched from what we were told was the Griffith Planetarium in the Hollywood Hills all the way to Mount Baldy in the east. Mount Wilson rose clear with its buildings and observatory almost directly to the north. When I stepped outside, sunlight shimmered on the white surface of the concrete road. I remember two things most. The crazy, tar-filled cracks jigsawing the road and the profusion of flowers spilling over garden walls, multicolored with enormous leaves. Then the smells: a strange, sweet smell of soil and tropical plants and the parched smells of dried grass, bleaching on the vacant lots.

Squinting up into the sunshine, I saw a large boy emerge from a hole in the bank of the road and shake off dust like a dog.

"You're new," he said.

Though broad and tall, he had a babyish face, his forehead green under the beak of a baseball cap. He wore cowboy boots and denim overalls with a T-shirt underneath. Within a week we too would be wearing T-shirts and Levi jeans, delighting at the ease with which we could crawl among the gravel and rocks or stagger to the imagined bullets of new cap guns.

"I'm Jimmy Stewart," the boy said. "Any resemblances to the movie star are incidental."

We introduced ourselves, grudging because shy, and Jimmy said that we talked strange, "real strange," but were welcome to see his chickens and rabbits. He acted at once as our self-appointed mentor.

From Jimmy's backyard the mountains opened out, tawny brown in the foothills, almost blue in the distant ranges, and Baldy looked as if it were covered at the top with snow, though we learned it was only bare rock glinting in sunlight. We wondered at Jimmy's clean hens—corrected to "chickens"—brown and shiny and taking water and grain from immaculate stainless steel containers. They lowered their heads and sat like cats in his arms when he picked them up. No less clean, the rabbits were quite unlike the stinking animals we had raised, and they too were gentle.

"They're not for eating," Jimmy said. "And they know it. I raise them for show in the 4-H program."

He explained how children could keep all

kinds of animals, even cows and horses, and show and sell them at special fairs. Jimmy had two guns: a pellet gun and the one we came to envy, a Daisy BB gun. He held his pellet gun with the barrel pointing downwards, but every few minutes he would raise the gun toward the sky and shoot.

"Chicken hawks," he said. "I get 'em every once in a while. I figure they're invaders with no rights."

We were glad to find out that Jimmy, like ourselves, had been an outsider too. He came from a farm in Iowa, where he had driven a Farmall tractor and done chores and where his family had raised pigs and horses. That was during the war, before he became a Californian.

I asked, "When did you come to Los Angeles?"

"Never. I came to Loss Angullus. That's how you say it. Ioway and Loss Angullus. Two, maybe three years ago. Me, I'm already a native."

Both of Jimmy's parents were at work when he took us into his house. Apart from the venetian blinds on the windows instead of curtains and the hard furniture with wooden arms and rough uphol- stery, the house seemed comfortable. In the hall stood a metal tripod holding a huge bottle labeled

"Sparkletts," from which, when we pushed a button, water gurgled down into paper cups.

"Los Angeles water comes in pipes," Jimmy said. "From upstate. We Stewarts don't trust it."

On the walls of the house and on the mantel and other shelves were pictures of animals, mainly horses. Jimmy told us of the Kellogg ranch, where we would go in a few weeks, and the beautiful horses there, describing them as if they were people living in a perfect world, but he talked slowly, casually, taking for granted that everybody saw things as he did. He appeared to us much older than twelve.

Jimmy seemed pleased that we knew nothing of his landscape. We recognized the name Kellogg, to be sure, but not from the Kellogg ranch. It was baffling how little we did know, how rare the familiar names when he spoke. He tested us about the Mojave and Sierra Madre, Topanga and Malibu, San Jacinto and La Brea. Thanks to the train journey, I had some sense of the whereabouts of the Salton Sea and Twentynine Palms. Yet why would swallows return each year to a town called Capistrano? Was there really a place called Death Valley, where eggs fried on overheated cars and where the land sank below the level of the sea? How would they be able to measure it? Was Jimmy joking about coyotes and roadrunners and wild bears in a park called Yosemite? And where was here: this unclosed warm place, so filled with color and deprived of color at the same time, so overpowering in its light?

9

When we came in for dinner that evening, we found Father dressed like an engineer, in loose overalls, with a thick blue shirt, and a pair of shoes that must have been Uncle George's because they made his feet large and ungainly. He seemed off balance, like a stranger in the house. Usually a careful dresser, who enjoyed wearing suits or jackets, he had the look of a different man, a man masquerading as my father.

"Daddy!" said June. "You can't wear *those* clothes."

"George wants me to go to work with him," he said to my mother. "Tonight."

I realized he was looking beyond my mother at Grandma, who looked down and said nothing. Nothing else was said at all, until George came into the room and, in his chesty voice, asked if my father was ready.

"We'll grab a sandwich or something on the way. All set, Jerry?"

After they had driven for a few miles toward the center and east of the city, my father began to smell what at first he could not identify. The smell of city dust he knew, even if this dust was peculiar, but something faint and rank came through as well.

"It's the slaughterhouse," my uncle said, as if thinking the same thought. "It slips in at night with the Pacific fog. You get used to it."

My father felt he never would. This was not his city, this muddle of trucking depots and dark streets, this deserted waste place with its smells of carcass and dirt. How could his own brother be at home here? George was explaining why the promised partnership involved my father's earning credit for his half, cleaning factory offices and accepting a limited salary until the brothers were equal partners. This was far from what my father thought he had been promised, so far that he felt he had no words even to begin to protest.

They stopped first at Ptomaine Tommies, for coffee and a hard roll with butter, for neither was hungry. Here the air was heavy with meat sauce and garlic, mixing with the moist odor of sawdust from the floor. They sipped the hot coffee drawn from a row of stainless steel urns, listening to a man named Luigi talk about what he called his nest egg. He wanted to go back to southern Italy to marry, taking his twenty-five thousand dollars in saved tips. His white apron had stains of tomato sauce; mechanically, he wiped the varnished counter with his cloth. He had been a night waiter in Los Angeles for twenty years, but home remained a village south of Naples, where Vesuvius was just visible. With only two hundred dollars left to feed a family, my father envied this man, envied his money in the bank and his chance to go back. Yet they shook hands on parting almost like friends.

George stopped his 1947 Hudson, the blue, two-door Commodore Six, bought in honor of my father's arrival.

"This," he said, "is where we start."

My father looked at the sign saying "Ceco Steel," at the long shed of a building, windowless except for the glass front doors and the small squares of opaque glass around them, now glinting in reflection of the car's headlights.

2 1

"It certainly doesn't look like much," George said, once again echoing my father's thoughts. "You'll get used to it."

Inside was worse than outside. The yellow fluorescent lights were tired and intermittent, the floor a black labyrinth around desks and tables and partitions. My uncle explained how the floor must be dust-mopped, then mopped with water and ammonia, then mopped again with wax, and finally buffed with the large polishing machine they had carried in from the trunk of the car. He gave instructions about getting water from faucets in the yard at the rear of the building. And leaving my father to his task, keys in one hand and a soiled dust mop in the other, he pushed open one side of the glass door and slipped out. The Hudson's engine broke the stillness, leaving it more absolute behind. My father locked the door. He felt alone for the first time in weeks, truly alone for the first time in his life.

When he went out to the back of the plant to fetch water, he stepped into a world of piled steel: I-beams and rods and plates, stacked like lumber across a vast, partly roofed area, smelling of rust and oil and paint. At last he found the water tap, but as he turned it on he realized that he had left the keys to the building next to the cleaning utensils and locked inside. Worse was his panic when the lights went out, engulfing him in blackness. He neither knew the way to the door nor had the means of opening it if he could find the way. His first impulse was to call for help, but he suspected there was no one in the neighborhood and that, in any case, a stranger would not be able to enter the building without his key. The yard itself was fenced with a high wire barrier, barbed wire strung across the top; he had seen a section of it as they arrived.

After holding on to the edge of the sink for maybe a minute, he knew that his eyes had adjusted as well as they were going to and that the dark was no less intense. He could see nothing. His only option seemed to be to find his way to that part of the fence closest to both the building and the road and wait for someone who would call the police. Yet the dark was so palpable that he could only guess about the right direction. Soon, too, he began to fear the possibility of a piece of steel stabbing his face or putting out his eye. With awful clarity he remembered his friend and fellow worker Jock sitting down one day to his midday meal on a board with a nail, which pierced his scrotum. The memory hurt as if his own renewed pain, for he was, he discovered, shivering with a physical dread, and there was no one to help.

He moved, one careful step at a time, hands in front of his eyes, groping his way through what seemed like a forest of iron boughs and needles. Finally, sweating and panting, he reached the wire fence where diffuse city light gave some visibility. Almost immediately, a car drove toward him, its siren barely growling but with headlights burning into his eyes. Out stepped two figures with their arms raised, telling him not to move. His mouth dry with fright, his fingers hooked on the wire fence, he found himself trying to convince two uniformed guards that he belonged there, belonged in that last place on earth he wanted to be, before they agreed to use their own master keys and let him back into the building.

"Why in hell is a white man like you doing a nigger's or wetback's work? Where are you from, anyway? Are you in the union? Listen, you'd better watch yourself around here."

When they left, joking with him now about his

accent and his bad luck, he continued for a time to work, still numb and occasionally shaking though no longer in a sweat. He could not tell how much time had passed, but George had not returned and he was only perhaps half done. The gritty floor, sharp with trodden steel shavings and worn to the quality of rough terrazzo, reflected light where it was still wet from the slime of wax. George had, he realized, forgotten to show him how to use the polishing machine, which jumped sideways when he tried to start it and knocked over a coat tree near the door. Soon he discovered that gentle motions, up and down, controlled the sideways rhythm of the machine, almost as if one rocked a baby, the electric motor humming a lullaby. He tried not to think of children, especially of his daughter who, she had told him several times, would not forgive him for coming to Los Angeles. Bad enough, but not as bad as his wife's remark when they arrived last night.

"I know I agreed, Jerry, but I'll regret this decision as long as I live. Please take me home."

If only, any more, there was a home. Here, where his mother lived, where his brother and sister had grown to be adults, where his father had died. Here had to be home. There remained no money to go back to England nor any job to return to if they were in England. Things were not much better now than they had been after his marriage, when he had been out of work for almost a year, before carrying bricks and mortar at the site of the Queen's Hotel. He had given up a good job to come here, and for what? Was this to be his partnership? He thought of the new national health program which might have protected him with a sick wife.

And he thought of something else, of northeast winds pushing up the slopes of Whernside, his children holding hands beside him, lying into the wind over the lip of the mountain. Far away a train puffed across the long viaduct, six carriages and a goods car, inching northwards. The wind was fresh and clean in their faces. His daughter was laughing and laughing more when the wind muted her shouts. Sheep cropped on the green slopes below them. They stood where Roman soldiers had stood centuries before, as high and as far away as seemed possible, and he had sensed that this image would return in moments of pain and nostalgia. He caught again the smell of slaughterhouse, mixing with the chemical smells of ammonia and wax. The machine was silent in his hands. All was silent about him. He sat down on the floor and wept.

§

On the day we sailed from Southampton my mother took to her bunk. She wouldn't eat and didn't try to get up. For my brother and me the *Queen Elizabeth* was a bonus paradise we had entered in anticipation of the real paradise in California. Staterooms with hot water and clean towels. Dining rooms with more food at one meal than we had seen in a year. Ballrooms so large they seemed a miracle in the confines of a ship, like the Pennine caves opening into unexpected chambers with shiny brown stalagmites and stalactites, except that here were fluted columns and floors soft with carpet. We ran down stairs, exercised elevators from top to bottom decks, sneaked into the stiff and silent world of first class. I ordered my first Coke in a spacious lounge, unsure what I would get when the starched waiter came smiling across with a tray and a glass for me alone. Then off to steam room or shuffleboard or the swimming pool that swayed and rolled like the waves outside.

The dining table was elegant, with thick white tablecloths and padded chairs. At every meal we were offered different kinds of apples: Pippins and Golden Delicious, Western Delicious and McIntosh, Rome Beauty and Cortland. It was National Apple Week. I loved the menus, with their pictures of ships and fruit, all tied with tasseled gold strings. But I couldn't understand them. There was a "recommended menu" and a whole extra page of alternative dishes, many sounding exotic, like a feast in fairy tales. "Filet de Plie, Duglère."

"What is it, June?"

My sister delighted in translating French, which she had studied for years.

"Just plaice. Like plaice and chips."

"And what's 'Farinaceous'?" My mother had to tell us later that that meant starch. We reported to her our experiments with "Pigeon en compote" and "Potage Condé" and the Rothschild pudding, having drawn the line at "Turkey liver en brochette."

"Please, children, no more about food. It's not a good time."

If my mother got sick early in that voyage, most

people followed at one time or another. After three days a black tropical storm began to move the ship at will, throwing her into holes or battering her rudely from side to side. The engines seemed to shudder and groan and thrash in pain. Smells of oil and bilge filled the lower decks. Up above there was vomit on the railing. Winds sang ghastly songs in the cables while the decks plunged and leaped back into the stinging spray, before plunging again into dirty gray waters. I sang to myself the old song we had learned in school about the mermaid with the comb and glass and the wrecked ship, unsure whether to be the captain or the cabin boy drowning in the storm: "And this night they will weep for me, for me, for me, and this night they will wee-eep fo-or meee."

It may not have been the most brutal crossing the ship had known, but the crew was saying so. People lurched on deck or bumped into each other in the corridors, those at least who stayed up. Settings slid across and spilled from tables. For two days I felt untouchable, until a lunch with creamed corn brought the awful realization. Even then, it was only after watching a sailor doubled over the ship's rail and retching passionately that I finally gave in. With my stomach emptied and my legs buckling underneath, I went to bed for the next two days. When I had strength to get up again, the storm had blown beyond us, and the big ship moved again with its gracious, slow roll toward New York.

"Did you see them?" my sister said one lunchtime. "Look, over there!" She pointed to a table across the dining room where I saw two black people, neither of whom I had noticed before.

"It's Ella Fitzgerald and Ray Brown! It is, I know." We never did discover why such famous musicians would be traveling cabin class, so close to us; but this was a big event in my sister's life, for she could sing many of Fitzgerald's songs. It meant as much as meeting Tom Holly and Con Martin and the other football players for Leeds United, people she had idolized for years. Now she could admit that America had some consolations.

The fifth day of our voyage there was a notice on the chalkboard used for news and ship's events:

"DEWEY LOSES. TRUMAN WINS PRESIDENTIAL ELECTION."

While I had only a vague notion about Truman and American presidents, I recognized the excitement and the surprise of the adults around me. My parents were disappointed that Norman Thomas, the Socialist candidate, had lost but were satisfied that democracy was at work in their adopted land.

As we approached New York, my sister and I stood early one morning, watching the flush of water along the dark, sweeping stern of the ship. As if at a signal crates of apples and oranges began to fall from the ship into the wake, gobbled up in white water, then rising again behind, as the sea-gulls swooped and screeched. We could not believe that food could be thrown away, especially fresh fruit, and we stared in horror as the kitchen crews pitched away what seemed to us pure treasure, crate after crate.

June said: "Think of Auntie Dot and Grannie—and Hazel!" (Hazel was her best friend.) "Why can't they have it? It isn't fair." She was crying. "It just isn't fair."

New York harbor had closed because of fog. Everything dripped gray and clammy and cold. Parts of the ship itself were lopped off or missing. We arrived and did not arrive, waiting, according to the chalkboard information, just out of the port in international waters. The ship put aside its elegance and beauty, taking on the character of a crowded bus station, with trunks and cases blocking the walkways. Shops stayed unlit and empty. Lounges turned into offices. The crew with different voices now gave orders about disembarking, customs, immunization. Passengers became less friendly, shuffling back and forth along the decks and packing the public area.

Our anxiety was more pointed. After fighting and getting scratched by my brother, I had developed impetigo on my cheek, and we were hesitant to treat it as usual with Gentian Violet ointment, which would discolor and draw attention to the infection. My mother was afraid that, if it showed any more, spreading beyond the Band-Aid given to us by the steward, we might be apprehended and held indefinitely on Ellis Island.

As it turned out, no one so much as looked at my infected skin, and even my mother and I forgot our apprehension when the fog lifted, as if to declare that we were ready now to enter the country and make our parade, horn blasting, by the Statue of Liberty. To me the statue appeared small and unimpressive, a miniature copy of my imagining. I was more engrossed by something I saw after we docked. Immigration officials unwound sausages from a woman's waist until she became, instead of large and smiling, small and angry like a barking Pekingese. I had no idea what language she used in shouting at the officer who remained to check the rest of her possessions.

§

After we had been two weeks in our new home, Vergil Smock called on the telephone. It happened to be my turn to answer the phone, and I picked up the heavy black receiver, saying—as I had been instructed to say:

"Albany 2690: the Dawson residence."

There was a pause and then: "Let me talk to Mr. Dawson, please."

Although I recognized his voice, I quietly passed the phone on to my father. By that time, I think we had almost forgotten him, but we were soon excited again, remembering the gentle talk and the free Cokes. He would arrive to pick us up, my father said, at noon tomorrow.

My brother and I rose early, already dressed in our new jeans and short-sleeved shirts, springing around in sneakers and feeling much older than we had when, wearing short pants, we sensed the amused looks of the other passengers in the railroad car. ("Railroad," Mr. Smock would say. "It ain't a railway in the States. Take me, I'm a railroad man.") Noon came without Mr. Smock; so did one o'clock, and two, and three.

"He won't come," said Uncle Bill, in his Big Bill Campbell way. "Nigras ain't reliable, can't be trusted. I'm with Strom Thurmond on this one. And if he does come it won't be a favor to them boys of yours."

At a quarter to four he did come, so late that we were by that time almost disappointed to see him, though pleased that my uncle was wrong.

"See, Uncle Bill, we knew he would come."

Vergil Smock came dressed for something formal, in a dark suit, with a tie. My mother said she worried at first that he might have been drinking, a matter she was sensitive about after a lodger had left our house two years earlier, his room a collection of beer and whiskey bottles. She explained later that Vergil was only shy and awkward away from the place where we'd met.

Sitting proudly in Mr. Smock's gray Plymouth sedan, we drove down Scandia Way, Avenue Forty, along Eagle Rock Boulevard to Colorado Boulevard, past Eagle Rock, which we had only seen from the distance, and followed Colorado along the edge of the foothills.

"Over there is the Rose Bowl," said Mr. Smock, "and that's Suicide Bridge. See how they put that fence around to stop people from jumping off?"

"Do people really jump from there?" my brother asked.

"Is the ocean wet? Check."

"Have you seen anybody jump? What do they do with the bodies?"

Mr. Smock smiled but didn't answer.

Once we had driven a few miles, Mr. Smock grew quieter. He stopped telling us about places or asking questions. We began to wind through less attractive areas, where refuse lay on the streets and large porches drooped like noses on the faces of unpainted houses. My brother and I agreed that this was not a pleasant part of the drive. It was long after that my sister told us that Vergil Smock had been driving toward his own house to introduce us to his family. Now he simply drove on without comment, neither enlightening nor chastising us. I know that he took us to Lincoln Park, an amusement park, but

I have no recollection at all of the place or the rides, only of the ca-thonk ca-thonk ca-thonk of car tires hitting the road joints as we drove down the Arroyo Seco Freeway to get there. Toward the end of our outing Mr. Smock asked us to name the streets we crossed by reading the signposts. Sometime he chuckled at our pronunciation, but usually he would look impassively ahead and say "Check. Uh huh, check."

When we got home, my parents were anxious. There had been questions. Why had they let children drive with a stranger? Didn't they know the risks? Couldn't they see he was a colored man? But my parents were confirmed believers in human decency who would not have worried without the prompting of our relatives.

"Won't you come in and have some tea, Mr. Smock?"

Vergil Smock had probably had enough of the odd family from England, and a glance at my relatives would have made clear to him the kind of welcome he could expect inside. He declined, thanked my mother, promised to come again, and, after rubbing my brother's head, drove away for the first and last time.

"What a nice man," my mother said. "Don't you think so, Grandma?"

"He's not so bad," my grandmother replied, "for a nigger."

❧

2

The Toland Way School came as a revelation. Instead of stone on stone, dark with soot and age, it was bright brick with shiny windows, its entrance surrounded by flowering bushes, and there were even camphor and pepper trees on the front lawn. Inside, crayon drawings of Spanish galleons, of Indians squatting near mud huts, and of cowboys firing six-guns covered several walls. The classrooms themselves were light and large, filled with bright maps and pictures, as well as more student drawings. All the blackboards were green.

At the beginning, Mrs. Brown's class was friendly, as if school were a kind of family and Mrs. Brown herself a solicitous and comforting mother, who welcomed me into her home. I heard that first day names like Cabrillo and Junípero Serra, Kit

Carson and John Frémont. Carson and Frémont like ourselves had crossed the wide country, entering what Mrs. Brown called the promised land and securing it for the United States. The Mexicans like the Indians had played their part, but the missionaries and rancheros vanished into ghosts of the past, and soon the real Californians came after gold and land, the best settling south of Tehachapi.

While proud of my own long journey and eager to love what Mrs. Brown loved, I had a numbing ignorance about everything from Conestoga wagons to giant condors. Mrs. Brown herself appeared to be uninterested in any history that was not American, or more to the point Californian, so that the past of other nations, however appropriate for those nations, had here an un-American, a useless quality, like the technology for a forgotten machine. Almost instantly, in this new classroom, I had no history, just a personal past that proved briefly curious to my new classmates, and it seemed to me that I could only adopt another history by forgetting what I knew. This was not so much a question of facts as of loyalties, and that first day we were expected to pledge allegiance to the flag of the new country. I felt awkward and self conscious, and my mother, when we talked with her about it, wondered whether we should refuse to participate.

"Oh, what's in a flag?" my father said. "We're here in another country, soon to be our country."

"So much the worse," my mother said. "So much the worse. Well, then, do as you think best, children, but I would *not* pledge myself to a foreign flag. To any flag for that matter."

Although for a time I chose my mother's approach over my father's, it didn't last. Mrs. Archer, the principal, called me in one day and, treating me like an intelligent adult, asked me where I intended to live and whether, "regardless of reasonable scruples," it would not make more sense to participate fully in my adopted country.

"Belonging," she said, "isn't hard in Southern California. Just remember, even the trees are imported here, and they took root."

In five minutes I felt almost eager to prove my allegiance.

Of more dramatic interest in the school was the lavatory, unlike any public lavatory I had ever seen, let alone ever smelled. To enter that cool basement was to smell clean, disinfected floors, to catch the luxury of crude and pungent, yet somehow satisfying, liquid soap, dispensed from glass containers that rolled over and spattered the sink with green spots. The only public toilets I had known were filthy places, where open troughs of urine lay stagnant, where finding a dry place to stand was futile, where paint peeled after a century of caustic moisture and abuse, and where water dripped from overhead tanks, the chains for which were broken or missing. Here instead was cleanliness and order: a rich whiteness of marble and porcelain, with hoppers that flushed confidently and doors that snapped shut on chrome latches. In addition to hot water, I enjoyed the paper towels, which seemed too good to throw away. Unsure at first, I left the slightly used ones on the edge of the sink.

In one of the sinks in the Council school I had tasted my first banana, scraping a little flesh from the inside of a speckled, withering skin as it lay discarded on the crazed porcelain. The flavor, which was bitter, set my teeth on edge. This was shortly after the war, and after years of reading about exotic fruit, breadfruit and passion fruit, pomegranates and bananas, the tasting of that skin was a furtive but exciting joy. Now I washed my hands before eating fresh oranges and bananas in any amount I wanted. My own lunch was fairly meager, but I was among people whose mothers provided thickly layered sandwiches, Snickers and Almond Joy candy bars, as well as cakes and fruit. With such riches generosity came easily, and while I fretted about my reputation as a scavenger, I ate with the hunger of someone who never quite had enough. Food emerged, too, from small metal lunch boxes, each of which had its own shiny, ribbed thermos, each its place on the shelf in the rear of the classroom. Until we begged these lunch boxes, I felt like a deprived as well as hungry alien. When we did get them, my brother and I, the meals we brought remained a basic peanut butter and grape jelly sandwich, usually sodden by noontime, made with slices of spongy, tasteless bread.

Still, that was better than the steamed food we had for lunch in Calverley, its foul stench overwhelming on rainy days. Brought in from kitchens in the town of Pudsey, it seemed always to consist of old cabbage and gray meat, with a rolled steamed pudding for the sweet. One day a week there was a reprieve, for we were allowed, if our parents gave us money, to cross the park to the fish and chips shop, where we usually bought dinner for the entire family, running home with delicious smells rising through newspaper wrappings: smells of hot fat and batter and fish cakes, which were layered sections of fish fillets and potatoes fried in batter. Shortly before noon on Fridays the teacher would ask how many students needed to leave early to pick up the fish and chips. All hands went up, regardless. Sometimes the teacher would check us, asking the details of our orders, but we were all prepared to lie even if we were running home to eat stew.

If our parents were not home, they might occasionally allow us to stay and eat the fish and chips at school, a special treat. Once I raced across the park, far ahead of anyone else, only to catch the worst part of a rain shower, which soaked me as well as my fish and chips so that I had to sit, wet and miserable, peeling bits of newspaper from the sodden food.

૭
In the New World people waited for rain. Every day the sun shone with the same intensity; mornings were dry and dewless, smelling of dust and eucalyptus oil, except where people hosed their gardens or sprinklers sprayed out overlapping foun-

tains in the early shadows. At recess we played a game called basketball, which had been a girl's game, netball, at home, but we also played tag, which was tig, and other games that were just the same. To rest we sat under trees in the huge, paved playing field, eating candies and cakes from cellophane packages. Instead of drinking water from a shared iron cup, always chained to the tap, we had the luxury of water fountains, which first shot up hot and then half-cold from chrome spigots.

School ended surprisingly early, at three o'clock. After school we walked home with boys whose names I forget, though I know that the one with red hair and freckles and ears that stuck well out from his head was to die as an officer in Vietnam. Sometimes we went with a group that walked up Division Street, across the hills to our house. Sometimes we joined others who went along Toland Way, the street below our own. This second route took us by several bare, round hills covered with the strawlike dried oats that grew on all the open land. One day, about a week after our arrival, we followed the other boys, picking up large squares of cardboard, torn from soap cartons, and carried them to the top of a hill. The slick grass served like winter snow, the cardboard like flimsy toboggans, and we slid at eye-tearing speeds down to dusty clay and litter near the road below. After one ride we were covered with the husks of the oats, which stuck to our hair and clothes, itching into the skin.

Soon we grew more daring and turned around on the cardboard to slide on our bellies, bouncing over hard clay and stones, our faces stung by the rushing grass. Without any pain I discovered that a piece of glass or metal had sliced the cardboard and my new pants. Underneath, the skin of my thigh had opened up like a flower, almost bloodless but wide and purple. Later I sat in the kitchen of our new home, shamed because I wore no underpants, while various people inspected the wound and, I was sure, glanced up my leg.

"Doctors don't come cheap. Besides, it doesn't look bad to me." I think my grandmother said this.

My parents agreed not to go to a doctor, and the cut festered, partly open and weeping, for months to come. The scar remained always.

"At least your cuts match," my mother said, pointing to the recent scar across the inside of my other knee. She looked away without continuing. I knew she was thinking of blackberries on the stone walls at home, where Mr. Matthews, the farmer, shouted at people to "get arter yon medda" (he meant out of his life as well as his meadow). In September I had been sitting on a wall and had fallen backwards through brambles, one of which tore the skin on the inside of my knee. My father used his white handkerchief to press against the cut, and I had lain down in the grass, looking through the leaves of a tree overhead, wondering if my classmates would be impressed. Now I sat on the red plastic of a kitchen chair, three or four people making tea while they talked around me.

"This will all heal," my mother was saying. "Here, love, have a cup of tea."

One day on leaving the Council school I had accepted Keith Bradley's dare to steal from Morton's Shop, which was on the same street as the school and known to be an easy target. Either I was too slow or the shopkeeper was too alert. His strong hand gripped my arm as he hurried me back to the school, dragging me by the time we got to Mr. Hayes's classroom.

"I nabbed this beezum stealing apples in my shop. I want him punished."

Mr. Hayes looked severe, looked as furious as he did when he heard us substitute our own words to "Waltzing Matilda" or "The Great Jehovah," and he said, ominously, to Mr. Morton that he would attend to the culprit immediately. A stern lecture followed about shame to parents and growing up with a firm sense of morality and property. Could I not know by now the difference between right and wrong? Finally, Mr. Hayes put me on his knee, patted my back, and told me about the beauty of apple trees, while insisting that I share his cup of tea.

"Let's just leave it that you are a good boy who has made a mistake," he said. "I won't need to tell your parents."

I sat there, afraid to speak or move, until the darkness had settled and he nudged me without ceremony toward the door.

"No more stealing, mind. Or a caning next time—and I *will* tell your parents. Run along now."

I remember a triumph in escape, a sense of his awful folly, for I knew that I would steal again just as soon as I thought I could get away with it. I remember, too, that it was spring, early spring or later winter, when traces of snow hid behind stone walls and pools of water lay in the greening fields. I could see little that evening, which was moonless and dull, but the smells of spring were there: new smells of turned earth and growing grass mixing with dank smells of rotten leaves. Suddenly as I ran from one lamppost to another, a car I recognized as a police car drove up from behind, and someone was shining a bright light at me and shouting "Hey!" Convinced that Mr. Hayes had changed his mind, or that Mr. Morton had taken his own measures, I started to run, ignoring the louder shouts, and cut across the nearby fields toward home. When I arrived, scratched and panting, the police car was waiting, and a policeman stood laughing by the kitchen door. It was my Uncle Tom, telling my mother about her son's running away.

"He took off, you should have seen, Lorna, like a thief in the night. Nay, lad, talk about a guilty thing surprised. Wot's on your conscience?"

Mr. Hayes may have been unusually forgiving because he thought of himself as a patron of the arts. Any pupil who could sing or paint became a favorite. I could write verses. When my parents decided to move to California, I felt at first only a kind of pride, knowing that my classmates would envy me. Soon enough I realized that if we went to California, I would miss the school trip to Scotland, so while I would not have given up California for anything (and scorned my sister for her folly), I still managed self-pity and something like mourning for the missed week in the Highlands. I wrote this:

> *Hoorah for the Grampians of Scotland,*
> *Hoorah for Ben Nevis so high,*
> *Hoorah for the heather blooming*
> *And the peaks reaching up to the sky!*
>
> *Hoorah for the braes of Lomond,*
> *Hoorah for Loch Katrine,*
> *Hoorah for bonnie Scotland*
> *That I have never seen.*

If it was longer by a stanza or two, it was not much better than what I recall. However, Mr. Hayes admired it, insisting that I read it to the assembled school. That part I don't remember, although I probably enjoyed the attention while hating the performance. What I do remember is the singing afterwards. To avoid punishment, we normally substituted parodies for the song's real words when Mr. Hayes cupped his ear to another part of the group.

That day in my pride I sang "Great Steamroller" for "Great Jehovah" at the moment he walked by. His face became a purplish red as he scowled and turned away.

Big faced, bald, as well as florid, Mr. Hayes was not Mr. Hayes to his school, but "Bungy." All our teachers had nicknames. Miss Shearer was "Kitty." Mr. Lunscome was "Bluebeard." Mrs. Armitage was "Bugwash." Bungy was originally Bunny, a reminder of his diet of carrots and vegetables, grown in his own kitchen garden, though "Bungy," which meant smelly, also fit with his love of strong cheeses. All of us knew, without admitting it, that he was a kind man, more inclined to forgive than to punish. Bungy himself knew that we knew. To make clear that he could be stern or to maintain his authority, he would periodically order canes from the local shop—light garden canes stained green, which snapped easily, although they could hurt a bare hand or bottom. If they weren't broken by the end of the first day, the canes ended up hidden by students on a ledge in the fireplace, where they could not tempt Bungy or Bluebeard into another caning.

We sang a song that owed its beginning at least

to the "Battle Hymn of the Republic" and that paid tribute to Bungy by a mock celebration of corporal punishment:

Gory, Gory hallelujah!
Kitty hit me with a ruler,
Bungy hit me with a walking stick
That made me black and blue.

I think there were also lines about Bluebeard, who loved to cane people and who came out of his torpor when there was someone to punish.

Kitty was my teacher that last year. She was an odd, angular woman: very tall, with an unbending and long neck and straight pale hair. I found her witchlike and frightening, because she would hover or sneak up behind us, pecking our shoulders with strong fingers.

"Inkwell, inkwell, inkwell. Fill it. Nib, nib, nib. Change it. Your paper is a disgrace."

Kitty would hold up an ink-blotched paper, pinching the corner with her fingernails, as if the thing were contaminated, and say with a pained voice:

"To whom belongs this egregious example of

sloth, this moronic insult to the world of letters? You children are a disgrace. A positive disgrace."

Kitty obviously hated to teach us, hated even the place itself. She stepped off the bus in the morning as if the conductor had stolen her fare. Without any special favorites, she had definite enemies, among whom Roy Gott was in a league by himself. One day, Kitty flashed into anger when Gott told her she should pick on someone her own size (actually Gott was her own size) and shook him so hard that his new bright green jacket tore along the back seam.

"A'll bring me mum to you," he said.

"Well, then, I shall bring my father to you."

"Me granddad's a farmer and A'll bring him," said Gott.

"Have him bathe first," said Kitty, "for I shall bring the headmaster."

Soon it was the local vicar and the owner of the mill, the County Council and the member of Parliament. Clearly enjoying himself, Gott ventured on the prime minister and Kitty countered with the royal family, and the exchange ended with Kitty shaking Gott and Gott shaking Kitty, both screaming, until Mr. Hayes banged through the door to frown on his teacher and to cane the rebel. We disliked Gott, who was a bully and who filled up the classroom with his smells of pigs and manure, yet we were in awe of his independence, and we never felt any respect for Kitty again. For myself it didn't matter. I sat in her classroom for only a few more weeks, and by then her pecking had almost stopped.

§

Mrs. Brown, who drove to school in her own brown Cadillac, from Glendale, was a plump, smiling lady, kind to most of the students and inattentive rather than mean to the other few. I think she would have been horrified at the idea of someone like Kitty, though she probably never encountered a student like Gott.

To commemorate the hundredth anniversary of gold being discovered at Sutter's Fort, she was telling us about the gold rush, about wagons rutting stone trails in the Dakotas, sailing ships floundering as they rounded the Cape, San Francisco Bay littered with abandoned hulks, miners battling in Angel's Camp and the rest of the Mother Lode country for claims and land and women. I was so excited by her stories that I decided I would write a poem. I presented it to her one morning, a little shyly, but proud and expectant.

"Thank you," she said, putting on her butterfly-shaped glasses. "What's this?" She read the poem and turned to me, and instead of looking pleased, she was frowning.

"Who wrote this poem?"

"Me."

"No you didn't. Fess up now."

She would not believe that I had written a poem and kept saying that my best response would be to confess immediately. She could easily find me out. Despite being falsely accused, I felt more guilty the more she demanded an apology, though I could find no words to clear myself.

"All right, young man, we'll try a little test. I want you to write another poem—let's see—a poem about clouds."

Humiliated but trying not to cry, I told her I had nothing to say about clouds. When she argued that obstinacy was a further sign of my stealing, I decided to write another poem after all, aware that writing could have different meanings. So I *wrote:*

53

I wandered lonely as a cloud
That floats on high o'er vales and hills . . .

It wasn't much of a poem, she said, and it didn't have a whole lot to do with the assigned topic.

"But I'm interested in the forty-niners, Mrs. Brown. Not clouds."

While grudgingly admitting that my second poem indicated I might have written the first, she remained suspicious.

Mrs. Brown's worst punishment may have been unintentional, except that I think she realized how miserable she made me feel and still chose to continue. As she took roll in the morning, she would ask us to say our names in order. My name was a straightforward "Carl Dawson."

"No, no," she would say. "Carrrol Doorson. That's how we say it in California. Once more now."

However much I twisted my mouth and tongue, I simply couldn't change my name, and after a few subdued attempts to imitate her, I gave up. This was not a matter of principle, because I envied my sister her ability to imitate anybody and to sound, after only a few weeks, like any other

Californian. I was just a poor mimic. Soon Mrs. Brown had the other children laughing at my pronunciation, with the result that any temporary advantage I enjoyed from my foreign birth became another liability, lumping me with the poor Mexicans Mrs. Brown despised, the wetbacks and fruit tramps and "Pachucos," or any other of the various immigrant groups who were despoiling Los Angeles.

Talking had long posed special problems for me. Until I was four, only my mother and sister could understand what I said. Even my father threw up his hands or turned, frustrated, to my mother for an interpretation. "Just what is the boy trying to say?" Probably a little worried herself, Mother took me to be seen by Dr. Bateman, to make sure I didn't have a cleft palate or some other physical handicap. It was after I had started school that I finally learned how or chose to speak in a way that others could understand. I had been sitting in Mrs. Lupton's classroom for about a month, when the class was talking, one day, about the river Aire and its sad travels from a place called Malham to the blight of industrial Leeds. It seemed time to speak. The river bubbles up, Mrs. Lupton was saying, at the foot of Malham Cove. To her surprise, I was waving my hand.

"Yes, Carl," she said, no doubt expecting my private gurgles.

"There's actually a system," I said, "of subterranean lakes. That's where the Aire comes out of." Maybe I had been silent, but I had also listened to my parents, and when it seemed necessary, talking happened on its own.

In Mrs. Brown's class I was learning a new language which seemed at once the same as mine and utterly different, as if there were a key to a foreign place made up of secret words and intonations, just beyond my imagining. Like Sinbad and his cave.

"I hope Carroll that you—and all your classmates—appreciate how lucky you are to be living in Southern California; and I say Southern California rather than just California, because in this promised land we are privileged to inhabit the finer part, *an island in the land*." (When Mrs. Brown talked about California she always sounded like a book.) "I do not except San Francisco, which is rapidly being outstripped by Los Angeles. What we have here is the world's most ideal climate, suited to fruits and vegetables as well as people. We produce more food in Los Angeles than is produced by any other county in the nation. Our problem used to be irrigation and is now immigration. Whereas in earlier times Los Angeles attracted the wealthy and the talented, it has, since the war, drawn from different sources, inside and outside the forty-eight states. This has its advantages in the way of our labor force for new industries, as my husband would argue. He's a developer in the San Fernando Valley. As for my own opinion, well, Adam and Eve didn't invite many visitors into Eden. Nor was there then a Communist threat."

Within a few weeks Mrs. Brown and I came to a kind of accord. Evidently wanting to treat me kindly without being able to, she devised a simple way out. She asked whether I might like to sit apart from the rest of the class and read, writing reports and doing the assignments on my own. So I slipped away into Jack London novels and Stanley's reports of darkest Africa and dog romances by Albert Payson Terhune (who made collies perform amazing deeds), along with the books—*Ramona* was the important one—that Mrs. Brown assigned me to read. In fact, I never finished *Ramona,* which didn't appeal to my need for exploration and physical trial or more dramatic heroism, although at the time I could become nostalgic for California's Spanish and Indian past and was willing to assume the best about Junípero Serra and the missionaries' treatment of the Indians. My most absorbing books remained *At Grips with Everest* and other Everest accounts and, to a lesser extent, the histories of Scott and polar historians: men (with the exception of a rare dog, they were all men) who reached the end or the top or an extreme point of the world, preferably with the loss of toes or legs or lives. I imagined frustrated rescuers mourning my own lonely quest and reading, as I lay frozen on the Rombuk Glacier or buried in an Antarctic snowhouse, my modest journal of suffering and adventure. "The world," they said to each other, "will listen now." In the new reading for Mrs. Brown's class, my favorites were the Richard Halliburton descriptions of exotic places and London's *Call of the Wild* and "To Build a Fire," which reminded me of the Everest expeditions and of heroes who failed.

Among the school friends that my brother and I made were the Danbergs on Verdugo View Drive, up the steep hill from our own house and diagonally across from Uncle George and Auntie Minnie's new house. Steve and Mike, who were almost the same age as my brother and I, soon invited us to play with them and their many toys, including electric cars, tether ball—which we returned to between every other activity—and pistol size BB guns.

Their house looked much like our house in size and furnishings, except that entering their house was an unsettling experience. First, we had to take off our shoes at the door. And when we padded in, Mrs. Danberg was sitting in the living room without any clothes on. I had never before seen a naked woman, and my brother and I were both embarrassed and near to giggles. But Mike and Steve accepted the situation so easily that we managed to be at least polite. Acknowledging our surprise, Mrs. Danberg later explained that she and her husband were uncomfortable in clothes and that he, especially, needed the ease of nakedness after a day in the office. Apparently, too, their reading of certain prophets—Blake was one, and Swedenborg another—had led them to conclude that while accommodation with society was proper, independence of spirit meant honoring the imagination through the human form. Hence a natural nakedness, as Mrs. Danberg put it. At home and in the nudist colonies.

Much as I tried, I could not keep my eyes off that large, white body. I was fascinated by the sheer bulk but also by its graceful movement, most evident when Mrs. Danberg hurried into her bedroom to fetch a robe or dress, to meet the postman or to buy from the Good Humor driver or to talk with a neighbor. It seemed miraculous that she could be the same person with clothes on that she was without them, and I think in a way she was not the same person. That may have been what her prophets had told her and what she was trying to explain to us.

At the back of the Danbergs' house builders were finishing construction, and workmen with bulldozers had left a large pile of soft dirt or sand, which they used as fill around the house. Soon our games included a running jump from the deck, still without a railing, far down onto the dirt pile below. One Saturday my brother jumped off and, with his usual daring, somersaulted in the air. He came down on his back and lay, twitching and in agony, like a wounded animal. I thought he was dying. Mr. Danberg rushed from the house with his dressing gown half on and looked with us into Paul's frightened eyes.

"He'll be OK, Carl. I've seen it before. It's just the wind knocked out of him. We'll wait a while to be sure. But boys, do me a favor. Go play somewhere else."

The Danbergs introduced us to Alden Baker, who lived at the end of their road. I associate Alden with two things: with my first grilled cheese sandwich, a delicacy his mother often made for us when we came to the house around lunchtime, and camping in "the canyon," which sloped down behind Alden's house. Actually, to continue up our street was to twist around the canyon and climb to Verdugo View where Alden and the Danbergs lived. We had already explored the canyon, which at the time had only a few houses around its western rim and almost none on the high and steep eastern side. A stream that failed by summer still oozed through lush trees, including a clump of bamboo, from which we made poles and spears. Where the trees grew tightly together, we could build jungle bungalows or disappear in elaborate games of hide and seek.

What made the place particularly inviting was the junk that had been thrown down from the road above—old refrigerators, tires, wooden pallets, chicken wire, car parts, sometimes tools or boards that were coated with gritty cement. These were all incorporated into Foreign Legion forts or lookouts against invading Nazis and Japanese (known as "Krauts" and "Nips") and the Commies, who had begun to emerge as enemies in England and were arch-villains to our friends but remained unpotent to my brother and me. The idea of an iron curtain intrigued me—or frightened me, like the image of iron lungs—and while I had seen pictures of the Berlin airlift in *Life,* it seemed odd to have the Germans as friends. We had been killing them throughout our childhood, shooting down their planes and inventing our own Normandys.

Alden suggested that we camp out one night on the eastern side of the canyon, at a point where there was a level area near an outcropping of rock. My parents were skeptical, having heard about the hermit who lived at the bottom end of the canyon and already worried, like most parents, about the polio scare. California had more cases of polio, the paper said, than any other region. Perhaps, too, they were apprehensive about our unplanned and total freedom, which seemed to spring from the new surroundings.

At the beginning of our preparations we made lists and agreed to assignments, then lapsed quickly into our usual disorder. We had planned to build a pirate cave, like the one that had collapsed and killed some boys in another part of the city, but our parents had forbidden any such projects, and we couldn't easily dig in the dry adobe. From the Danbergs and from Uncle George, Paul and I borrowed sleeping bags. We took prepared food with us, since fires were not allowed, and pitched camp in the evening, which meant that we argued about the best location for the sleeping bags. Alden, being so close to home, demanded first choice, promising to run across for food and, late in the evening, for hot chocolate and marshmallows, when the air grew cool and damp.

We sat up late, singing advertising ditties that we all knew:

Pepsi Cola hits the spot
Twelve full ounces, that's a lot,
Twice as much for a nickel too
Pepsi Cola is the drink for you.

And songs that some of the boys had learned in Woodcraft Ranger camps:

My gal's a corker, she's a New Yorker,
I buy her everything to keep her in style.
She wears silk underwear, they cost ten bucks a
    pair,
Hey boys, that's where my money go-oh-oes.

Alden talked about girls bleeding each month from a kind of penis pipe, and how his mother, who appeared to me a Florence Nightingale of sandwiches, was in truth a bitch. It seemed strange that he could be so angry about such a person, and I thought how lucky he and the Danbergs were to have mothers who could prepare such food for them to eat. Then I thought about Mrs. Danberg's naked body, which didn't seem to fit with Alden's attacks on girls and menstruation (a word that I knew but didn't speak) and which made me feel a little like a traitor. Alden reminded me of my cousin David, a few years older than I, who always wanted to be the leader, and who bullied others into silence by saying what no one else quite dared to say.

"There was this guy, see, who got a flat tire and had to stay at a farmhouse. His name was Fuckerarda. . . ."

I woke in the morning feeling uncomfortable, as if irritated by the sounds of novel words. A whitish mist spread over everything, erasing even Alden's house on the other side of the canyon; the trees looked ghostly and distant just a few yards away. I was tempted to waken my brother in the eerie stillness, but I lay quietly in the sleeping bag, rubbing my legs to keep warm. I felt that something was going to happen and fought to keep from blinking. Slowly out of the fog, trotting up from the canyon floor, I saw what appeared at first to be a dog, a limp chicken dangling from his mouth, his head slightly angled away from his body. He came directly toward me, then stopped a few feet away. I knew from my reading that it was a coyote. After staring at me for just a few seconds, he changed his path, swung around our campsite, and vanished into the mist.

Intimate with the code, Mowgli would have spoken to him, and he to Mowgli.

"Greetings, wolf child. Killing is the coyote's law. The morning is good, is it not?"

"Good it is, great hunter. What news of the jungle?"

But with the coyote silent and gone, I faced a morning that was not good, with no one to talk to and with a sense of nothing to say. I remembered the Everest climbers, Somervell and Irvine, freezing in their tiny tent above camp seven, unable to go up or go down, waiting for the storm to pass, if it ever would. They suffered together and talked through the long night. And I remembered my own camp in our backyard when the rain came and the tent began to leak. Instead of staying out through the night, I knocked on the door and woke my parents so that I could sleep in a warm bed. Saddened with that old awareness of failure, I felt empty and useless, farther from Everest than ever before. I concentrated again on the coyote, and only then did I think to shout and tell the others what had happened.

"Heck," said Alden, "seeing a coyote's nothing. I do'd it all the time. Besides, if you really saw one, where is it? Bet you made it up."

"I didn't either," I said, already knowing but disliking the routine.

"Did too."

"Didn't."

"Prove it."

The only proof I could think of was to find the owner of the chicken, which Paul said may have belonged to the hermit, who lived close and whose fences were bad. For some reason Alden agreed that this made sense. So when we had dressed and eaten our cold cereal, we walked down the canyon to the hermit's house. It wasn't a house so much as a tar-paper hut, surrounded by tires and other junk, as though after great rains the whole canyon had flooded and deposited everything here, in the hermit's yard.

"His name's Mr. Berry," Mike said. "He was a schoolteacher. They kicked him out for being a drunk. All he does is collect trash and go to the store for more wine." Under his breath he said, "Any winos home?"

And then he yelled, "Hello! Anybody home?"

Shouting was not a good idea, for a snarling, mangy-looking dog leaped up at us from the camouflage of surrounding junk. Luckily he was on a chain, which tightened around his throat and sprung him back, away from us. He lay down again as if we didn't exist. After maybe half a minute, Mr. Berry pushed aside the burlap feed sacks which served as his door. He was a short, raggedly dressed man, with a bushy white beard and long, straggling hair. Apart from the gallon wine bottle he carried hanging from his finger, he resembled every picture of a hermit I had ever seen in books.

"What's up, boys?"

Alden explained that *we* had seen a coyote with a chicken in its mouth and wanted to know if he was missing a chicken. Mr. Berry laughed and squinted at the junk around his house, as if to say: "How am I supposed to tell?"

"Coyotes come through here all the time. My responsibility is to provide them with meat."

Then he glanced around again, like someone who had never seen the place he lived in, rubbed his dog with his foot, and went back inside.

"OK," said Alden. "This is the protocol, the law of the canyon. Secrecy and silence. We all saw a coyote, and it took a chicken from the hermit's yard. Feebleweaks tell on pain of death."

Under the hay the smell is stronger, moister, and the light dusty and dim, almost like a church. We have burrowed into Mr. Matthews's haystack where we talk of illustrious deeds and knighthoods. Peter and Keith Bradley, Beryl Webster, my cousin David Hardcastle, and my brother and I. David has just explained why he should be King Arthur, sending the rest of us on errands of mercy while we look for Norma Johnston, his ideal of the beautiful girl, or any other girl, he explains, with big breasts. Out of nowhere we hear a bulllike roar, loud cursing dulled by hay. Soon the ribbed ceiling of hay buckles and pitchfork tines stab through from above, grazing David's leg. He screams as the pitchfork disappears and plunges again, jabbing this time into a wooden board. Only now do we appreciate that Mr. Matthews has discovered our hiding place and cares as much about his territory as we do. As if one person, we leap through the thin cover of hay that masks our entrance and sprint by the farmer, who curses us as if we had poisoned his best cow.

"I know you buggers, I know you," he shouts, but his pitchfork is stuck in the haystack and we escape, laughing and frightened, to the nearby woods.

"Next time," says my cousin, "I'll stand in a tree and piss on him when he comes by."

"We weren't hurting his hay," says Keith Bradley, "only playing."

"Bloody bugger," says my cousin. "Look at my bloody leg."

The outer tine has torn the skin, and with his leg stretched out on dry leaves, blood drips through the hairs of his thigh. David is a few years older than the rest of us. He has hairy legs and his voice has changed.

"Bloody bugger. Bloody farmer. Bloody hell."

We all begin to laugh again, unsure how to respond to David's language.

"I won't piss on the bugger next time, I'll shit on him. That's what I'll do. I'll stand in a tree and shit on him."

The next day we returned to the haystack and scattered hay as far as we could, throwing it into the air, then kicking and stamping wherever it landed. Within a week David had fulfilled his promise of aerial urination, but it was Keith Bradley, not Mr. Matthews, who walked innocently beneath the tree.

It seemed odd to want escape from the sunshine, which was unremitting and tiring by mid-afternoon. Paul and I had found the cool basement of the house, the small door unlocked, and it turned out to be a cavernous storage area in the wedge-shaped space between the hill and the lower floor. When our eyes had adjusted, we recognized boxes and trunks filled with pieces of cloth. My grandmother had worked for many years as a seamstress, and she either had used enormous amounts of material, leaving the remnants here, or had bought the remnants to be used later. Almost the whole space was packed with cloth.

Uncle George had told us that his mother was a talented pack rat, who collected everything.

"Do you know that your grandma sews for Hollywood film companies?"

We did not. It seemed unbelievable for her to be associated with anything that exotic. Over the years she had sewn all sorts of costumes and had even made the harness, said Uncle George, that Harold Lloyd used when he swung from the gigantic clock in a movie that we had seen in Rodley Cinema.

There was something irresistible about opening huge trunk lids and making nests in the musty cloth. We were apprehensive after Jimmy Stewart's warnings about black widow spiders, which Jimmy said could sting us to death, and we reminded ourselves of the story my mother told about the young woman at a wedding party who hid in a large chest. Once inside, she could not move the latched lid, and no one found her until her lover discovered the skeleton many years afterwards. Such risks added to the pleasure, especially when we pretended to lock each other in, sitting on top of the trunks and ignoring the sounds of appeals through muffling cloth. We hid in the trunks for whole afternoons, listening to sounds from the house above, to the buzz of the traffic, or to the noises of children at play, elsewhere in another kingdom.

After a few weeks, Grandma realized with horror that we had violated her trunks and boxes, and she forbade our entry into "her" basement. That didn't stop us entirely, for when she left the door open or we found the key in her sewing room, we managed to sneak into that cool, dark space, and all the more happily after we both confessed to hating our grandmother.

"How do we know she is our grandmother," Paul said. "How could she be? She doesn't even like us. Besides, she left our dad when he was little."

I thought of Grandma Dawson, who was my father's grandmother, and who had raised him after his parents immigrated. By the time we sailed for America, she had a white film over her eyes and could barely see, and she hugged me, smelling of tobacco and old furniture. Tea in her house tasted of condensed milk, but it was strong and sweet. Grandma Dawson was proud of my father and said that she had another baby—that was Auntie Nellie—"to keep him company" when his parents left.

He was only four when they sailed for New York. They had been small-mill owners, who had lost much of their money, they said from theft and police corruption. The United States promised to be another good beginning for my grandfather, whose parents were Polish Jews and had come to Yorkshire a generation before. They planned to settle somewhere in America and to send later for their son, but they never fully settled. Nor did they send for him. After losing money in the leather trade in Rochester, New York, they set off first for Seattle, then for Los Angeles, where their last important choice lay between buying property on Signal Hill and buying a small house in Highland Park, once a flourishing center for writers and artists, now a decaying suburb. They chose Highland Park. This was 1921, within months of the discovery of oil on Signal Hill.

Grandma Dawson, who, as my father put it, "shared a house" with her husband, was forced to clean one of the new Leeds cinemas in order to feed her grandson and the new child she bore, at forty-seven, to be his sister. When the Great War came, my father's chances of seeing his parents diminished further, and by 1918, neither his parents nor his grandmother mentioned the plan of sending him out to America. He took his grandmother's name, perhaps out of affection, perhaps because it sounded more English than the name of his parents, and in school his friends renamed him "Jerry" after a famous goalkeeper. So instead of Cecil Jacklin, he became Jerry Dawson, growing up in Leeds rather than Los Angeles. He was nearly forty when he saw his mother again, and his new brother and sister were themselves in their mid-thirties. By now his father had been dead for several years.

"Maybe Grandma murdered Granddad and

buried him in one of the trunks," Paul said. "That's why she doesn't want us in the basement. I love Grannie Woodhouse and Grandma Dawson but I hate Grandma Jacklin. If I'd been Dad I wouldn't have come to live with her. I think we should kick her out of the house."

9

To visit Grandfather's grave we had only to cross the valley, for the eastern stretches of Forest Lawn faced Grandmother's house, its grass the only bright green grass in the area. Most peculiar about this trip was that, in the warren of roads and slopes, chapels and statuary, we never did find the gravesite. Grandmother's habit of staring down gave her no spatial sense at all, and Uncle George would have nothing to do with what he scorned as barbaric burial practices. He wanted to be "burned," he said, and preferred that Minnie, his wife, be thrown in after him, Hindu style. When he said this, my parents stared at him with puzzled expressions. I knew he must be joking because he turned to me, raised his eyebrows, and winked. Then he chuckled, insisting that he neither knew where Grandfather was buried nor cared any more than Grandfather himself did. What mattered, he said, was to show us all the statue of David, one of the seven wonders of a corrupted world.

"This is what Michelangelo would have done," he said, "if he had had the taste and decency of these preservers of our loved ones, not to mention their money and influence in Sacramento."

He pointed straight at the large fig leaf covering David's crotch. My mother, not pleased, stepped quickly away. She would speak openly if reluctantly about matters of sex or about the body, but she could never listen to this kind of joke.

"Well," said Grandma, "his grave is somewhere here. It's just like him to get lost. We'll come another time."

Except for Grandma's own funeral, three years later, that remained the only time. But we continued to look across at those green slopes until my parents bought another house farther along and on the other side of the street.

I came home one day to find my mother sitting in the living room with two men, who looked like and turned out to be undertakers (or morticians in our new vocabulary), wearing dark suits and handling, with no apparent purpose, large tape measures. Both men talked fast and earnestly, taking turns in addressing my mother, who smiled and gestured for me to sit down next to her. With her usual kindness, my mother had invited two door-to-door salesmen from Forest Lawn to enter the house. No one else was around. The men pretended to greet me, which gave them an opportunity to repeat their pitch. They were authorized to sell newly developed Forest Lawn plots for a special price, which was available that day only. Additionally (said the second man), these bargains of the day were actually view plots, pointed at Mount Wilson. My mother lifted her hand to stop the talking.

"Let me be sure," she said, "that I understand. You have what you call 'plots' available on a special basis, today only, and the best feature of the plots, price aside, is that they have a view. May I inquire whether you provide periscopes?"

The two men looked at each other, looked back at my mother, who remained unsmiling, and both began to snigger, then laugh, and laugh so hard that they started to cry. When they had folded up their notebooks and advertisements and wiped their eyes with handkerchiefs, my mother asked them if they might like to join us for a cup of tea.

"When I'm dead," my mother said to me later, "I don't want to be buried, either. I think I'd like my ashes scattered in some pretty part of the Yorkshire Dales. I'll have seen enough of Mount Wilson by that time. Now I'd love another cup of tea."

༄

Almost as soon as we arrived in California, Uncle George talked about a Thanksgiving trip he had planned to San Diego. He hoped to visit a friend with whom he had served during the war. Grandmother didn't like the idea, as she kept telling us, but she said that if we wanted to save her the cooking, it was all right by her. Squashed again into two cars, we drove down the Arroyo Seco to Chinatown, through the downtown area, and were soon on Whittier Boulevard moving south. On the outskirts of the city there seemed to be endless telephone poles, with wires crisscrossing to the horizon. We also saw our first oil derricks, black and ugly, and pumps rocking up and down like horses on a carousel. Occasional houses sat next to derricks or on their own in the dusty, open land, looking temporary and forlorn. But within a few miles we entered avenues of lemon and orange groves, bright green trees stretching away in strict, geometric patterns, the foreground for distant mountains. Far to the east, a fire on Mount Baldy pushed clouds of smoke into the sky, like a volcano, but remote and unthreatening.

Sitting in the back seat I would close one eye, watching the signs: grapefruit and oranges for sale, fresh tomatoes, last chance for gas, someone's animal farm with giant pythons, Rancho del Mar. And the Burma Shave ditties, one little sign after another, zipping by in bursts of words, and ending with their triumphant BURMA SHAVE! regardless of what came before.

> *Beneath this stone*
> *lies Elmer Gush*
> *Tickled to death*
> *by his*
> *shaving brush*
> *BURMA SHAVE!*

It was impossible not to read them, at least for someone who read anything printed, whether books or cereal boxes or license plates.

I don't remember whether we drove through Anaheim and Santa Ana on the way down or on the way back, but I see them as small, almost toy towns, surrounded by farmland and orchards. We came to the Pacific near Laguna Beach, where the road followed the coast, the water dull blue in the morning light. A few people walked along the beaches. I can see San Juan Capistrano and Carlsbad and Cardiff-by-the-Sea, villages with tiled roofs and eucalyptus trees, sunbathed, lazy, inviting. At a gas station with flowerpots we stopped for a Coke, which came out of a bright red and rumbling water chest holding cold bottles like bowling pins.

When we arrived in San Diego, we wound up a steep driveway to a squat wooden house, from which we could just see the distant emptiness of the ocean. My uncle's friend, Ray, made everybody feel that the journey was a present to him and his family. He even shook my brother's and my hands, as if we were special guests. Thanksgiving, he said, was football day, and he threw us passes with a hard leather ball on the back lawn. At dinner we were served the largest turkey I had ever seen, and the first cranberry sauce, as well as the first yams and avocados and pumpkin pie. It would be long time before I could eat the mushy flesh of yams and avocados.

Ray's house was filled with model ships, mainly freighters and tankers, along with some sailing ships and one battleship, which had been based in San Diego. He talked a lot about the war, and he asked my father what he had done during the war. I noticed that my father paused.

"Exempted from service. They wouldn't let me enlist."

"Jerry did essential telephone work," my mother said.

This seemed unimportant to Ray, who just wanted to reminisce about *his* war. He and George had met in the merchant marine, and several of the models around the house were replicas of ships in which he had sailed. He spoke about convoys to Archangel, Murmansk, and other places I had to find later in the atlas, places to which he had journeyed in the boiler rooms of lurching, sometimes unseaworthy and ice-encased ships, targets for U-boats across the North Atlantic. Uncle George said that the Liberty ships, built in two sections, often had to be jacked up in order to fit together, and that with any sort of impact they could spring apart.

For years afterwards I endured nightmares of entrapment in the heart of a torpedoed ship. Steam

8 1

and spewing oil would scald my skin while the room filled slowly with churning water. Only in my waking dreams could I save myself and the ship and carry on to Archangel or beyond. Sleeping I coughed and burned in futile struggle, certain there was no escape.

My uncle told a story about two identical twin brothers, one of whom had good eyesight, the other poor, so poor that his eyes looked demonic through the thick corrective glasses. (George smiled and tapped his own thick glasses.) Both brothers had served in the merchant marine. What George loved about them was their interchangeability. The brother with the bad eyesight was a gifted swimmer, and he passed the test each year to be a lifeguard, then passed it again for and as his brother. No one could tell the difference except the brothers themselves—and maybe the person who needed rescuing from the water, for the one brother couldn't see and the other couldn't swim. It was "hap," my uncle said, that the swimmer died in one of those Atlantic convoys. He wondered why neither he nor Ray had kept in touch with the other man.

I wondered about my father and Uncle George and how close they felt as brothers. They looked like brothers, and I knew my father liked George more than my mother did, however angry he was about working for him. Even so, I couldn't imagine them swimming or taking a test for each other.

My father began to speak about our war: refugee children coming on trains and buses from London, to be farmed out to welcoming families; rations that were never enough and that were often not available to the prescribed limit; the bombings in Leeds and Pudsey, which lit the night sky, after the Germans had flown in at sunset from the Irish Sea. He told about Yeadon Aerodrome where planes were repaired in long, camouflaged hangers, and how we would walk by and wonder that such fake cows and barns could fool anybody. Uncle George said it was because the Germans, like the British and Americans—and probably not the Italians—only allowed men with perfect sight to fly the airplanes, while it was only the color-blind who could "see through" camouflage from the air.

I remembered as they spoke the big, lumbering bombers, Lancasters and Wellingtons, fighting for altitude over our rooftops, with the china rattling and windows and doors shaking in sympathy. And I remembered V-E Day, when all of that ended but nothing else did. The food was still the same, the errands for cereal or cigarettes, and my cousin David Hardcastle coming over from across the street to borrow sugar or something else that my mother had carefully kept for the end of the month. After too many requests my aunt would send a neighbor boy, a substitute for David, to try to cadge a cigarette:

"CanyalendMsssardcasselcigret?" Usually my mother could, or did, rarely to get it back.

§

I associate David with the end of the war, because in a way he defrauded us of our celebration. We had been given old rattan baskets, wool containers, by the owner of the mill in Calverley, and these, with dead trees and railway sleepers, we piled in a precarious heap for a bonfire—something far grander than the Guy Fawkes affairs of November. The fire was to be lit at seven-thirty in the evening, after tea and around sunset. Already when we came home from school, the fire was burning, had been burning for some time, and while David Hardcastle was nowhere to be seen, we all knew, intuitively, that he had come home early for his own bonfire. Later we discovered that he had singed his hair and was hiding, not from conscience, but from vanity.

As usual my mother saved the evening. I had been feeling especially bad because I had been spanked for breaking the blade of my father's bow saw the day before, and to have the fire burn without me seemed like double punishment. My mother came down the hill with a bucket of potatoes and explained that the fire had burned to the perfect point for roasting. So we threw the potatoes into the bright coals and smelled the scorched skin, cursing David to be sure, but glad that he was not there to enjoy the fire and that we would soon be eating one of our favorite foods.

"Sometimes," my mother said, "things do work out for the best. I also found a little margarine."

3

Hating dressing dollies;
Rather race and run;
Silly games that girls played
Really weren't much fun.
Much preferred a bicycle

To any other toy.
Yes, when I was a little girl,
I wished I'd been a boy!

A memory not my own becomes my own. A young girl, my mother, jumps across railway tracks, dances around the nettles and burdock, a newspaper package of bread and cheese and cold sausage in her right hand. She wears a soiled yellow dress and has a ribbon of the same cottony material holding her dark hair. She runs hard along the riverbank to an old iron bridge where her father, my grandfather, stands watch. The girl blurts out her news about the battle at Passchendaele, near Ypres, where most of the young men from her village have been fighting and dying, and her father sets her down, strokes her hair and asks her to start again.

"'Wipers' again; it's always Wipers. Or its bloody salient, 'where our gallant boys. . . .' Now, then, what's going on?"

Those answers, breathless and excited, remain unheard; only the murmur of that swirling, filthy gray river and the humming of insects come across the years. My grandfather nods and makes a scathing comment about British generals and about

Douglas Haig in particular. He looks up at the rusty bridge he is supposed to be guarding and then looks eastward, as if to the guns and the waste of Flanders.

"They didn't learn from the Somme. They won't learn from this. The bloody butchers."

He shares his meal with his daughter, who was to remember most her damp dress and bottom from the dewy grass. When she leaves, my grandfather stands again, his blue policeman's uniform immaculate as ever. Convinced that no Germans will ever deign to attack this bridge, he thinks about the futility of any attack and senses the futility of his own posturing, which extends beyond his present assignment. When—as another war called for further guarding of England's bridges—he was told about the cancer in his colon, he turned away from friends and family, refusing to eat, waiting impatiently to die. Now in the fading image of my memory he smiles as his daughter gambols away to the canal bridge. She has just learned to whistle.

❦

I watched her half asleep, half painfully conscious, her face puffy from steroids and crumpled like paper from the cigarettes that were killing her, her head scarf slipping higher on her bald head. The year before she had written:

When I was young my hair was thick,
Shiny and straight and long;
I liked it that way
But my sister would say
That to have straight hair was all wrong.

This would be my last time to see her, and she knew it as well as I. Did she sink into sleep to avoid me? Or was she simply too exhausted to stay alert? Whenever she woke up for a few seconds, she smiled, shyly adjusted her wig, and thanked me for coming.

❦

(I look away in panic and see my sister and myself riding a bicycle along the New Road toward Horsforth, a village three miles from home. Mother has sent us, or sent June, to fetch cigarettes, which are not always available and which someone may have seen in a shop in Horsforth. Against my parents' standing prohibition, we ride together on June's bike, and as we freewheel down by the river bridge, we hit a stone or slip on the shoulder of the road and are suddenly lying on the roadside, scratched and dirty and angry at the imposition. Neither one of us speaks, but we rub sore spots and fight back tears.

"I'm not going to smoke when I grow up," I manage to say to my sister. "You send your children out to get hurt.")

꿍

I damned silently the doctors who had brought her back from what would have been a final coma, granting her these few extra months of tortured consciousness and indignity. She had called with the good news that the lesions had disappeared from her head, but neither of us mentioned the lesions in the lung. That was three months before.

I smiled back. At last, when it came time for my father to drive me to the airport, I hugged the poor, thin skeleton that was or had been my mother and that was too weak to respond except with one light squeeze. I found no words to say to her, no words at all.

§

My mother grew up in a small house, with three brothers and three sisters, the youngest of whom died of polio. Her parents came to dislike each other, and her brothers hated their father. She would tell of one night in the kitchen when she found her mother with a bleeding nose and closed eye. Her brother Frank had taken a large carving knife and crept, like a savage in a Tarzan film, toward his father, until Tom and Leonard held him and his mother begged him to put down the knife, swearing that she loved him and was unhurt, that she had fallen on the table. Soon both were sobbing, while my grandfather turned away, bitter and alone.

My mother worshiped her father without understanding his violence, his coolness, his irony and disdain for those around him. She was also proud of him, this man who could eat raw tripe and gamey meat, who had entered the constabulary at sixteen, lying about his age, who quoted George Bernard Shaw and Joseph Conrad and Thomas

Hardy, and who had the kind of self-possession she could never find. Although a Socialist, he had been asked to run as a Conservative for public office, which he considered a wonderful joke. He had no desire for any service beyond that required by his work.

Unlike her brothers and sisters, my mother went on to grammar school, winning a scholarship from Salt High School in Saltaire, which was named for Titus Salt, the "philanthropist," who built his own mill, school, hospital, housing, and town. My mother was not only a good scholar, she was a strong athlete who captained the netball and hockey teams. In her own words, she "could run like the wind."

When she came to leave school she had—like my father—the chance to go on to a teacher training college, her one opportunity to become a gym mistress. To her lasting dismay, her father thought that the token five shillings per week were too much to spend and insisted that she work in the mill. She did, for three days, until the local headmaster sought out her father and announced that if Charlie Woodhouse didn't take Lorna out of the mill, he would do it himself. She left the mill but found only a poorly paid secretarial position, which made the mill seem munificent by comparison, and which required the expense of a bus ride into Leeds. Here she had to work for a smelly older man, whose foul breath and occasional touch would, as she often said, make her shudder for the rest of the day.

My parents met in a cycling club, the escape for each from the grime of Leeds. For years they rode with other enthusiasts to distant parts of Yorkshire. In those days people visited the Dales, but the roads were usually empty, and it was the dedicated hiker or cyclist who reached the remoter places. My mother admired the long, straight limestone walls rising from gentle river valleys—Wharfe and Aire, Swale and Nid—up the scarps of fells, across bog and high land as far as eye could see. She loved to watch the rabbits and sheep and to hear the sounds of curlew and plover, the names of which seemed to invoke the songs of the birds.

Before she died, she asked my father that her ashes be scattered on the moors near Malham, an area that remained in some profound way the center of her world, though she had never lived or worked there and spent the last thirty years of her life in what she described as the urban wilderness of Los

Angeles. Malham was the place she came to dream of when she no longer wanted to leave the confines of her house and habitually drew curtains against the sun. Even after she had stopped reading in the last years of her life, she returned to a little book called *The Flying Yorkshireman,* which described another misplaced kinsman, who suddenly found, near Santa Monica, that he could fly—a gratifying accomplishment for the homesick and exiled soul.

4

When Mother was ill one weekend, Auntie Madge and Uncle Bill invited Paul and me to stay with them in their house near Monterey Park. Auntie Minnie drove us over. She was a big, rangy woman with a very loud laugh. She came from Virginia, and my brother and I soon associated her with a song we had learned in school:

> *Way down south in old Virginnie,*
> *Way down where the cotton grows,*
> *Had a mule her name was Minnie. . . .*

Aunt Minnie sounded a little like a mule, at least when she laughed, and though handsome, she had an angular solidity that made the lines from the song appropriate. Uncle George also said she was inhumanly stubborn.

I remember arriving at Madge and Bill's house to see dates falling from date palms on the roadside. Unlike Scandia Way, their street was lined by trees and had the settled quality of an established neighborhood. Inside, the house was plain but welcoming, and Madge invited us to drink a Coke at the kitchen table. Almost as soon as we sat down, Minnie brought out an envelope filled with photographs of a sort I had not seen before. They showed her parents after death. It was hard for my brother and me to express much enthusiasm for pictures of unknown, shrunken people in coffins, and it was probably hard for Madge and Bill as well. After a silence, Madge said:

"Oh, Minnie, what a lovely coffin," pointing to a photo of Minnie's father.

"Best of all," Minnie said, "the coffin's fake. Can you believe we rented it? All you do is pay a little more for the extra doodahs. You bury the person—part-way. Then the mortuary pulls up the fancy box and leaves a regular box behind. Everybody's happy, 'cept maybe Daddy, but he'd be ornery anywhere, bless his heart."

After Minnie had driven away, Auntie Madge took us to Sears, Roebuck to buy roller skates. We had seen other children skating along the sidewalks near their house, roaring down the pavement arm in arm or in human chain or singly on one skate.

"Come on," Madge said, "You two look like born skaters."

The skates we bought fastened to the soles of shoes with clamps, tightened by a large key, much like a clock key. At first we were tentative and wobbled and grabbed trees or each other, but we learned quickly how to accelerate and turn, although stopping was more of a problem. Apart from scuffed knees and elbows, we skated happily all afternoon, jumping over cracks in the concrete ("Step on a crack, break your mother's back"), angling down driveways to the road, rolling into the hard, shorn grass on neighbors' lawns. It was maybe the first time in this new place that we escaped entirely from sickness or foreboding. We were not only left to ourselves but urged to play as we wanted, as long as we wanted.

Before taking us back the next morning, Auntie Madge made for us our first hotcakes with syrup, thirty-six of which we had eaten when she suggested that we might not want to burst or get sick in the car. Both of us felt that we could have eaten more.

On the way home I remember noticing how billboards loomed above the rooftops or dominated the streets, forcing me to read. Massive smiling faces spoke like comic book characters into balloons of type: "I've discovered the larger, finer cigarette. Pall Mall." That was my mother's substitute for Woodbines, and I already disliked the long, red package and the strange raw smell of its burning cigarettes. My mother smoked Pall Malls the same way I ate sweet foods, which was nonstop when they were available. She insisted on calling them "Poll Moll," as if to use the English pronunciation.

"Pell Mell," Uncle George said, "as in haste and London roads." My mother remained stubborn on that one.

At least the Pall Mall ads were better than the Camel ads, which had a dotted letter "T," called the "T Zone," drawn over someone's oversize mouth to indicate taste. Or those of Forest Lawn, with the

Wee Kirk o' the Heather or some other chapel announcing peace or joy or comfort. It seemed odd that they would advertise for people to die, especially since they had misplaced Granddad.

§

The roller skating at Auntie Madge's reminded me how much I missed my bicycle, which we had sold before leaving England. When we got back to Scandia Way I asked my father whether it would be possible to get a new bike, perhaps one of the sort that Jimmy Stewart owned, which had wide tires and back-pedal brakes, and which seemed a real western bike, designed for jumping ditches or racing down banks of adobe. Jimmy's bike was spotlessly clean and had a large sheepskin cover on the padded seat.

"Well," my father said, responding as he would respond for a long time to come, "we don't have the money now. You know that the trip here was terribly expensive, and it will take at least a year or more before I can buy my share of the business and earn the money we need. On the other hand, I know you want a bike, and you should have one."

Rarely if ever in times to come would he admit

that he could afford anything. It was impossible to know when he was really without money and when he was protecting what little he had.

"Do you remember our trip together?"

I did, probably better than my father. It had to do with bicycles, and when he asked, his bike came immediately to mind. Whatever kind of bicycle my father owned when he was young, the bike he had after the war was most unimpressive. In the first place, its colorless muddy paint had neither shine nor emblem. It was a German bike, and my father pretended to have captured it from an airman, whose Messerschmitt crashed on Beamsley Beacon, a hill near Ilkley. My brother and I had inspected the crashed fighter, and after arguing about it, we doubted that the narrow and cramped space could hold a bike. Still it was a German bike.

Tall and somehow gaunt-looking, its tires splayed out against the floor, my father's bike sat most of the time among the paint and tools and broken furniture in our shed. In preparing for our trip, my father wiped off the dust, carefully oiled the chain, put a few drops of oil in the nipples of the rusty axles, pumped up the tires, and tested the back-pedal brake. My own new bike, the best birthday present I ever received, shone by contrast. It was jet-black with gold insignia announcing "Raleigh Sports" across the horizontal bar and down the vertical pole beneath the seat. I was particularly proud of the three-speed Sturmey-Archer gears and the bright chrome of the lamp holder jutting beyond the handle bars, which had, unlike my father's bike, articulated handbrakes mounted underneath. The rims squealed when I drew on the handles, and the bike would stop as if to a secret command. I could also sound the bell as I pedaled along.

It was to celebrate the new bike that my father and I took what I believe was our only trip together without the rest of the family or a family friend. We went to Malham, thirty-three miles away. Usually our trips to Malham required the train to Skipton, changing for my favorite station of Bell Busk, with its flowers and the swallows nestling in the eaves, before walking the last few miles to Malham itself. This time we rode through Calverley, down to Greengates, across to Guiseley, where we ate fish and chips at Ramsden's, then on past Menston and the insane asylum (which always made me a little anxious, even though a family friend worked there), to Ben Rhydding, Ilkley, Addingham, Bolton Abbey, and Grassington, from which we left main roads and climbed over the farm roads the last few miles. On the very tops of the hills the road turned to grass, and we had to open farm gates as we rode along. Each gate seemed a milestone, a sign of my growing up.

That night we were to stay at the youth hostel, where we ate a meal of sardine sandwiches and tomato soup. After dinner we walked up to Malham Cove, strangely overarching in the dusk and more mysterious still when I learned of primitive peoples who had lived and farmed there thousands of years ago. Stone Age people seemed to belong in a land of stones and cliffs. I imagined them hunting animals across the windswept fells, digging the earth with flint tools, shivering in their cold and lightless caves. With my father nearby, it was good to curl up in the hostel dormitory, pedaling again to this wild and haunting place.

Our room on Scandia Way was heated by a cast-iron gas stove, which for my brother and me was irresistible. For the first time in our lives we tested paper matches, one of which would poof a flame of gas, before the flame crept, blue and red, across the ruffled face of the stove. No rooms except the living room and parlor at home had fireplaces, and to make a fire required an elaborate ritual of rolling newspaper, chopping and placing kindling, wigwam fashion, then carefully building the usually cheap soft coal, which smoked for minutes before reluctantly starting to flame. That was when we had coal. During cold winters when the supply was poor or our coal bin empty, we would gather sticks in the woods or walk along the railway tracks looking for odd pieces of coal, or hope, as sometimes happened, that a stoker would heave a shovel of coal from a passing train. Along with heating ourselves, we needed fuel to heat the water, which only happened when a fire was burning in the main room.

In our new home we had unlimited warmth as well as hot water. Just as ice cream stayed cold in the freezing section of the "fridge," and fruit ripened in neighbors' gardens, so heat poured immediately from the hissing gas. Even when the evening was still warm, my brother and I would fight about whose turn it was to light the fire. Sometimes we lit it over and over again, until by brother screamed and my father, angry and soulful at the same time, would pounce into the room and silence us. We were at once antagonists and friends in a space that was not yet our own.

At that time Paul, who was eight, could have passed for a boy several years younger. My parents had taken him to Dr. Bateman and a specialist in Leeds to see why he didn't grow. (Once at least he had worms.) Dr. Bateman said he would grow when his body remembered to. Paul was friendly with anyone who never mentioned his size or lack of it, but he would fight boys far bigger than himself at the least provocation. We two fought almost daily. I would tease him and he would flash into anger, and I would hold him at arm's length or pin him on the floor, until he yelped with neck-tingling cries or broke loose and scratched in frustration. Often as on the *Queen Elizabeth* his scratches gave me impetigo, which, since he never got infected himself, he chanted about with his own sort of voodoo, saying "Scratch scratch. Gotcha."

Our room was larger, lighter, and less damp than the bedroom in Yorkshire, where the beds felt to have been out in a blizzard, and where we shivered, sometimes for minutes, before the sheets grew welcome and warm. At home we had gone upstairs to bed. Here we went downstairs, which seemed odd and backwards. Another big difference between the old room and the new was that now my mother rarely visited us after we had gone to bed. In the old house she would come up to tell a story, or—much better—she would dress in a sheet and flutter ghostlike up the stairs, threatening us in a raspy voice that made us laugh and shudder at the same time, until she swooped into the room to pinch and tickle and it was time to say goodnight.

Our room in Los Angeles was furnished with two trundle beds, a scratched tallboy, and a treadle sewing machine. It also held an old wind-up gramophone, the needles for which—small steel points—we never replaced but used in a kind of rotation over and over again. I still recall the words of the few vocal records: "Twas on the Isle of Capri that I found her, Beneath the shade of an old walnut tree . . ." and "Red sails in the sunset. . . ." By the hour my brother and I wound up the old machine, plonked down the curved swivel head of the tone arm, and listened to the half-blurred and oddly distant sounds. "Oh, carry my loved one home safely to me."

When we weren't playing with the gramophone, Paul and I had two other favorite nighttime activities. The most satisfying was listening to the tiny Silvertone radio provided by Uncle Bill, who worked for Sears, Roebuck and who had given us the radio shortly after we arrived. It was about four inches cubed, with a loose wire for reception, and to hold on to that wire at night, lying under the blankets, was to will the Lone Ranger or the Green Hornet or Sergeant Preston (of the Northwest Mounted Police) into the room, announced by their soon familiar musical themes. In Yorkshire we had all listened at ten minutes to seven to Dick Barton, Special Agent ("Eeet woood be betta too deezpose of you now, Anna"), and for a long time I was puzzled that all Eastern Europeans bore the name "Conrad." However compelling, Dick Barton like Children's Hour was a public or at least a family event. The Lone Ranger and Sergeant Preston arrived for our ears alone, the faint, hollow, and tinny sound of our radio essentially private and exclusive. "On, King, on, you huskies!" Preston and his dog, who visited a town with our family name, made us part of a larger clan. We lived in the Yukon or galloped away, acknowledging the admiration of the less courageous: "Say, who is that masked man anyhow?" And off, astride white horses, to more adventure across the sands of the West.

We hardly needed the radio for some of our imaginings. For years we were the two brothers Bill, train engineers or soldiers, creating our own stories of runaway trains and split-second rescues, nudged by radio adventures or the compelling images from films. Our dramas also bred their own language, or at least vocabulary, which demanded for some reason high-pitched voices and crisp authority. (One phrase we used was "quine haben hunt," its meaning understood implicitly in our make-believe regions.) During these moments there was no rivalry, no fighting. It was as if the two of us needed only the language of another world to be friends. We would switch roles and power to imagine each new account, driving our trains at reckless speeds wherever we decided that evening to lay the tracks. With special trains, tracks could be ignored altogether.

Sometimes our journeys were re-creations of

real journeys, and we enacted again our coming to America, or the trip, now a year before, when we went to Liverpool for our visa. Since the American consulate wanted their own doctor to examine us and had given us appointments early in the morning, we could not arrive in time by train, yet we could also not afford to spend the previous night in a hotel. This meant that we had to travel by car, which my father had rented from Holesworth's Garage. The car was a blue and white Austin, about as large as Dr. Bateman's pre-war Buick, which remained to me the epitome of cars, and it was pure joy to see it turn up our street. I had ridden in a car only two or three times before and never any great distance. Once Mother's friend Nancy had taken us to Bolton Abbey for a picnic, but a cloudburst followed by flash floods had made that trip terrifying, stranding us as we waited hours to cross washed-out roads.

It rained on the way to Liverpool, too. My father had hoped for a beautiful outing, driving through the part of Yorkshire where my mother was born—it may have been Nether Thong—then over the moors into Lancashire. Because we were late, my parents decided not to look for my mother's birthplace, but my mother quoted one of her little poems about her early life, written, I believe, for us as children.

> *I was born in a street called Orchard Street,*
> *A ridiculous name I'll be bound,*
> *For no apple or cherry or even a pear,*
> *Was anywhere there to be found.*
> *The house was of stone*
> *With a flagstone floor;*
> *In winter the snow blew under the door*
> *Where the flagstone was worn with the tread of*
>   *feet,*
> *In the house where I lived on Orchard*
>   *Street. . . .*

I was relieved not to see Orchard Street, the area being so overwhelmingly ugly. All the towns in the area lay dreary and shadowed by clouds that hid the tops of mill chimneys and lights burning in the small, cramped houses, and it didn't seem right that my mother came to life there in a cold, drafty house.

Over the moors we could scarcely see, and my sister and I both got sick from the winding road. We drove down into Lancashire along a brackish, swollen stream, which sometimes splashed the road and

1 0 7

sometimes disappeared into a yawning valley, and my father, who hadn't driven since before the war, negotiated the narrow pavement hunched tensely over the steering wheel. The towns of Lancashire looked no more or less depressing to me than the uglier parts of Huddersfield or Bradford, but Manchester was different. Two years beyond the end of the war, it remained, as I envision it, a sad memorial, whole city blocks filled with rubble, houses incontinent without a side wall or roof, straggling bushes and weeds growing where people should have lived.

My sister, who had come to Manchester by train a few months earlier to participate in a Children's Hour sports quiz, recognized buildings and other landmarks and urged us to look more generously at the city she knew. No one else shared her enthusiasm. Driving through that battered and forlorn city seemed to give my father back a lost resolve.

"This," he said, "is why we have to leave England. All of England is as dead as Manchester."

He had worked in cities like Manchester during the war, installing repeater stations, signal-strengthening units, for the GEC, which operated the national telephone system. Posted for a time in Sheffield, he went back to his lodgings (he called them "digs") the evening of an immense bombing raid. When he returned in the morning, the entire street was rubble, and the repeater station, finished the night before, had disappeared totally. His job kept him out of the armed forces but took him into dangerous areas. Once he was thrown to the pavement by a bomb blast, which showered him with splinters of glass. He remembered the road bouncing him like a small object and a noise, which, he said, seemed to swallow all things and all meaning. Because of his travel, we saw relatively little of him during the war. Only when he was temporarily reassigned to Leeds could he stay at home and spend much time with his family. It was then that he would escape with us to the Dales, wandering over lonely fells and moors, which had imprinted us like fish in natal waters.

Hiking on Pen-y-gent one day, the weather hazy and warm, we were longing for water or anything else to drink. My sister and I lingered irritably behind while my father and brother strode on about a quarter of a mile ahead. Out of the ear-filling silence of the afternoon came my sister's excited shout:

"Carl! I've found a pen." Then, almost hushed: "Do you think it might be a bomb?"

For years we had been drilled to look at found objects with skepticism. Just as loose lips sank ships, careless handling of various items, above all fountain pens, could sink us. Dozens of posters, in school and out, had told us so. My sister stopped close to her find, hesitant to move, for there would be no way on barren moors to find again the identical spot. She shouted, then screamed, at my father, who was disappearing over a distant rise and who at first didn't hear. When we both yelled, he turned at last, obviously not understanding and reluctant to come back. In the end he did make his way back, and when he saw the pen, he shared our apprehension.

"All right, children, get far enough away."

How far away might be enough we could only guess. We went maybe forty yards from the place. Ignoring my father's motions to lie down and turn aside, we watched his tentative approach to the possible booby trap. First he took his knife and cut a long sprig of heather; then he lay down next to the pen, reaching slowly until he could turn it over. At that point I shut my eyes.

"Come and get your fountain pen."

It was a shiny, black pen, unbroken and apparently unscratched, its gold nib and clip as perfect as a new pen's.

"Look, Daddy, it's a Waterman."

"Mind you," my father said, as we set off once again, entirely revived, "even the Germans wouldn't be silly enough to drop booby traps on these hills. Bicycles no doubt, but not pens. I would personally have preferred a glass of water."

Another day we had to take cover in Kettlewell from a thundering rain, the only shelter the arch of a bridge over the river Wharfe. Unluckily, a dead sheep lay rotting in the middle of the dry space, so foul-smelling that it was almost preferable to stand in the rain. That was the first time I had seen a carcass covered with maggots, which looked like a living flesh beneath the parted wool. My mother refused to look at the carcass, but I could not avoid looking. It seemed to me that we all smelled of rank wool and decay through the long bus ride home, and it took weeks before I stopped thinking about worms or maggots nibbling on my own body and about the empty holes in that sheep's head.

§

The war had been a fulfilling time for my mother, who found suddenly that she could be useful and productive as well as independent. Since most men were directly involved with the war, jobs became available that would otherwise have been impossible for women to find. My mother started to work for Smith's Cranes, a large factory only a mile or so from home. Grandma Woodhouse, her mother, lived in our house during those years and helped to care for us as well as the house. After a short time at Smith's, my mother became clerk-of-the-works, with responsibilities and challenges, and for two years she worked happily in her new position. When the war ended her story was that of so many women—after this war as after the Great War—who were expected to return contentedly to their homes and families, torn from what had proved meaningful in their lives.

It was in the years after the war that my mother became ill. Doctors said first that she had given her children too many of her own rations during the war and suffered, as a consequence, from malnutrition. And perhaps that was a part of the mystery. She developed circulation difficulties in her legs, which became intensely painful. Neurologists and other specialists prescribed a range of treatments, including a spinal operation that would have laid her up for a minimum of six months. She refused the operation. By the time my parents considered immigration to California, her health had become a chronic and deteriorating problem. Not only was she physically ill, she began to have times of bitter depression. She would cry for no apparent reason, or stay in bed on days—like Christmas— when we wanted her most.

I remember one bleak postwar Christmas when she simply couldn't get out of bed. Usually a cup of tea in bed had made a big difference. We would brew the tea, placing it with a packet of cigarettes on a little tray. With one eye almost open, Mother would sit up, pulling the bedclothes with her, light a cigarette from the bedside table, then sip the milky tea.

"Ahhh," she would say, "thank you, love. This is the ticket."

That day there was no ticket. Neither tea nor cigarette would help.

My father had made us a fort, complete with lead soldiers, horses, and cannon, which he had cast and painted himself. Paul and I loved the fort but cared mainly for the drawbridge, because it opened and closed electrically and buzzed each time we pressed the button. When the battery died after an hour or two, I ran out into the garden and cried. Christmas was over. I felt like an orphan.

I went down to the playfield at the bottom of the street, for that was where we all went when we needed somewhere to go. Most days I preferred the swings, which we used as airplanes, leaping from the wooden platforms at the top of the arc and falling, twisting back to earth. Today I pushed the roundabout, an old steel contraption with rotting wooden seats, used less to spin around on than to bang back and forth like an open bell, and I chimed my Christmas glumly in the dampness and the cold.

𝄞
It's Leroys for Christmas joys
Gifts to bring you cheer,

1 1 4

No down payment, easy terms,
Buy now, pay next year.

Christmas started early in Southern California. Already in November the radio was playing Christmas songs and carols, as well as counting down the "shopping days" until December 25. At first I did not recognize the difference between advertising and ordinary songs. Doris Day seemed always to be singing "East is east, and west is west, and the wrong one I have chose," on the stations my sister liked, especially KFI, with its top-forty lists and its odd gong, which went BOYIIIIING! to announce new hits. Between the hit songs there boomed other harsh lyrics, drumming with uninterrupted and disorienting rhythm.

Tick tock, tick tock, time to shop
At your downtown department store,
Eastern Columbia,
Broadway at Ninth.

Other kinds of stores had competing music, including the new equivalents for chemists' shops. "Sa-von Drugstores, Sa-von Drugstores" sounded like an awful chant or incantation, different from "Music City, Sunset and Vine," which I didn't understand, but which always seemed promising. I liked the idea of a musical city, and I expected Sunset and Vine to match the Emerald City in the *Wizard of Oz*.

My brother, sister, and I enjoyed thinking about Christmas, because our aunts and uncles were already asking what we might need or want for presents. Thanks to rationing, we had few clothes in England to start with, and luggage restrictions had limited us to even less than we owned. What made matters worse was that hardly any of the clothes appropriate for the climate in Yorkshire were of any use in Los Angeles, except maybe short pants, which, as my brother and I soon discovered, nobody else wore. My sister had only one dress suitable for her high school, a school which she said measured everything by appearance.

> *Eagle Rock High School, cream of the crop;*
> *Our clean campus will keep us on top.*

Having always worn a uniform before, June felt especially uncomfortable. A further disadvantage to apparent poverty was the response, generous in its way, of some of the other students. One girl took pity on her, suggesting she would never fit in with the top groups on campus unless she wore cashmere "sweaters" with skirts. She even invited June home with her to see her clothes. Her house was a cramped, one-bedroom apartment, shared by her mother and herself, where, as if for a museum, she collected cashmere sweaters. Her mother proudly brought out all thirty-six sweaters in paper wrappers from their places on the shelves, unfolding them like silk kimonos. June was the first girl from school she had invited home.

It was obvious to me long before she described the problem that my sister was wearing makeshift uniforms, alternating a brown skirt and sweater one day with a plaid dress the next. Much as she hated to complain, she would sometimes grumble to me or even cry. My grandmother, after promising to make June a dress, evidently forgot to take measurements. After two weeks, however, she announced that June and I were to accompany her downtown the next day, a Saturday, in order to buy a dress. We were both excited, June about her dress, I about seeing the city, and we got up almost as early as Grandma herself.

The easiest way to get downtown by public

transportation was the streetcar, which stopped at the bottom of Avenue Forty and went a roundabout way into the city, ending up in Inglewood, many miles to the west. Bright yellow and green, the streetcars seemed freshly scrubbed after the Leeds trams, which looked as if the coalman had spilled his sacks on them. Surprised to see no conductor, we placed fifteen cents in a machine that whirred and rattled, sorting out coins for the driver to stack in a money holder. We drove down the middle of the boulevard, along raised tracks like railroad tracks, before turning left on Verdugo Road and on down, through industrial areas, to Los Angeles.

"I just realized," my sister said, "that we live the same distance from downtown Los Angeles that we used to from Leeds. But there we were in the country, here we live in the city."

"It is a sort of country," I said, thinking of the hills and the nearby canyon.

"Yes," she said, "it's both. Curiouser and curiouser." She started to laugh and to sing in my ear some of the hymns she had been learning.

"What about: 'I'm going to speak to Jesus on the royal telephone?' Or 'Drop kick me Jesus through the goalposts of life?' Imagine what Hazel would say to that one! . . . Don't you just hate trams—or streetcars. I do. They remind me of Roy Birkett."

Roy had been our neighbor in Brookfield, the County Council housing area where we lived in Yorkshire. His mother was known to boast equally about Rex, her dog, and Roy, who had begun to work in Leeds. One day when we came home Mother said there had been a nasty accident. Roy had ridden his bike into tram lines, tipped over, and had been crushed by a tram. For a long time afterwards I tried to picture myself caught for a moment and lifting up the front wheel to escape, or going across to Mrs. Birkett to tell her that I had found a way to save Roy, who was not dead after all.

"It's all right, Mrs. Birkett," I would say. "All Roy has to do is take his weight off the handle bars and pull up the wheel and race to the side. There's no need for him to be dead."

Downtown Los Angeles was filled with people, most without jackets or coats, walking slowly and waiting, like trains, for the arms of the traffic signals to lift or fall. Apart from City Hall—white as opposed to the black city hall of Leeds—there were few tall or impressive buildings. The department stores on the other hand were a kind of miracle, filled with merchandise of every sort and color and requiring no ration cards.

In the Broadway, June soon found a dress she liked, but so at about the same time did Grandma, who explained to June how good a dress she had discovered, and since it happened to be on sale, how much of a bargain. June said that while she liked that dress, she preferred the one she had found.

"I can wear it more often, Grandma. Yours is beautiful, it really and truly is, but I think mine will be more practical."

"Have it your way," Grandma said, snatching the dress June had chosen and marching to a cash register to pay. "No one listens to me, and I thought you were different."

Grandma said little after that, except that we were going to Clifton's, which was a cafeteria made to imitate a grotto. Taking just cottage cheese and a cup of coffee, she called our attention to the high prices and told us to pick dishes we wanted from the long counter. I felt overwhelmed, not knowing what to choose early in the line and what would come later. Still it was fun to eat in a kind of cave and to see my sister so happy.

From then until she moved into her own apartment, Grandma remained unfriendly to my sister and rarely spoke to her. That evening, when we had finished dinner and June had washed up, I saw her pour greasy water on the dishes June had washed.

§

It was soon after our trip downtown that Grandma, who maybe wanted to undo some of the damage she had done, decided to give Mother an early Christmas present. June, Paul, and I were in the kitchen one morning, making our breakfast and brewing tea for everyone else. Grandma pointed to a double-size Hills Brothers coffee can and winked and pointed again, impatient that we didn't understand her meaning.

"What is it, Grandma?"

"You'll see soon enough. It's for Lorna."

We began to have some idea when the can shook and a faint whimpering noise seemed to follow. None of us knew what to say or how to tell Grandma either that Mother was afraid of animals or that animals like humans had need of air. When my mother came into the kitchen, Grandma pointed once again to the can and said, without elaboration:

"Christmas present."

"Oh, thank you," my mother said, only half awake. When she opened the plastic cap of the can, a puppy, larger than the can itself, shot up like a jack-in-a-box, lathered and gasping, while my mother screamed with shock. She never managed to accept that Grandma had intended the dog for a present. "Smoky," as he somehow became—though black rather than smoke-colored—failed to grow into a normal dog, but wandered around with one ear draped over his head and spent most of his time in search of food. My mother would not permit him in the house.

❧

$\frac{1}{11}$ of the Nation's market . . . that's California! Last year the average Californian consumed $308 worth of groceries, 40% more than the national per capita rate of $220. With 9¾ million healthy appetites, California this year will represent a food market of more than $3 billion—big business in which every food grower, manufacturer, and distributor should be interested.

1 2 2

"Perhaps so," said my mother, responding to this (or a similar) blurb from a magazine that my uncle was reading out loud, "but I fail to see why eating should be a sign of quality or gluttony a matter for state pride."

Uncle George often quoted such passages, usually from advertisements, and my parents would complain, not only that he had been sending them this kind of material for the last two years, as if to make them dissatisfied in England, but also that it seemed like needless taunting of people who were unhappy or who had come, as my father began to say, under false pretenses. My parents wondered how George could be so skeptical about everything else and such a salesman about Los Angeles, as though he presided over Sunkist. They no longer wanted to remember the extraordinary packages of food he had sent to England: the dates, figs, chocolates, canned (my mother still spoke of "tinned") fruit cocktail, and the sweetened condensed milk. It was as if he kept reminding them of what they were determined to forget.

Food may have become unimportant, if not repugnant, to my mother, but to me, as to Smoky, it became almost everything. Along with the feasts at school, I ate whatever was served at home, accepted food from friendly neighbors, and found an entire source of new food on my own. On Eagle Rock Boulevard stood Robert's Supermarket, a kind of store unknown to us in size and offerings, where there seemed to be an acre of produce stalls alone. The fruit had color and freshness that were hypnotizing, and I would watch clerks cull the blemished fruit and sprinkle the heaped displays of mangoes or plums or cherries, along with the rich green leaves of cabbages and lettuce, of which there were many sorts. My parents said, no doubt rightly, that the vegetables and fruit lacked flavor by English garden standards, but the range was astonishing to us all.

Much as I admired the fruit, my favorite part of the store centered on the doughnut machine, tucked inside the rear door between the produce department and the rest of the groceries. Doughnuts were a new and addictive food. We would watch the rings of dough splash into rich brown fat, bubble and roll for a few minutes, before floating to the surface to be taken out. The perfect rings were sorted, some remaining plain, some dipped again in sugar or various sorts of icing or coconut shreds or crumbs. Any imperfect—and some of the no longer fresh—pieces were thrown away, except when children happened to be around for charity. I happened to be around a good deal of the time. That sweet, oily cake flavor drew me like nothing else, and I would eat doughnuts until my stomach hurt. It was the manager rather than the Board of Health who finally put a stop to free food, probably to get rid of parasites like myself who interfered with paying customers.

Robert's Supermarket served another purpose for us. We learned from Jimmy Stewart that soft-drink bottles could be brought to the market or to the neighboring liquor store for refunds. Two cents for small bottles, five for the large ones. For some reason, there was an almost endless supply of available bottles, lying on the roadsides or nestled in the weeds: Pepsi and Coke, Nehi and Dr. Pepper, Royal Crown and Hires.

"Los Angeles," Uncle George would say, "is peopled by loose bottles. Just ask Sister Aimee or the Forest Lawners or the Swami Paramhansahyoganandar atop Mount Washington." For a long time I thought he meant the bottles we collected.

Often the bottles were smoke-colored, having lain in the hills through the last winter, when city crews had come to burn the dry and flammable oats. Many of the bottles we returned were dirty or discolored, no joy to the storekeepers who had to hold them for the beverage companies and handle them with their other materials. They might grumble and, occasionally, refuse to accept our gatherings, but most of the time they were good-natured and tolerant, even when we borrowed one of the red steel Flyer wagons from a friend and could haul dozens of bottles in a single trip. For us the bottles offered an unexpected source of money, maybe the first money we had earned, my brother and I, allowing us to buy comic books or food at Jodi's hot dog and hamburger stand.

Jodi's was a special place. Sitting on a small, smooth concrete pad it was a kind of shrunken diner, with rotating stools under an awning on the outside and Jodi and his cooking fixtures on the inside. The structure itself was the size of a capacious outhouse, except that its skin was polished steel. On the inside of one wall Jodi had pinned a greasy photograph of "Miss Grill," who had served up six hundred frankfurters in an hour and wore a crown of franks, like feathers, around her head.

Jodi worked with room at most to take one step

to his left or right and to pivot from back to front. There he prepared cheese sandwiches, hamburgers, and hot dogs, brewed coffee, poured cold drinks, and talked his own soft and nonstop drawl, while reaching food out through three different windows to his customers. He served drinks in funnel-shaped paper cups that fitted in metal holders. Hamburgers were wrapped in white paper, from which the shredded lettuce always spilled out. Squeezed between the independent liquor store and the supermarket liquor store, the place was popular with market customers, storekeepers, policemen, streetcar drivers, and most of the local children. No one made better hamburgers than Jodi or served Nehi and Coke so deftly. No one's prices were any lower. Hamburgers, fifteen cents; cold drinks, ten. From a distance, Jodi looked like an overweight Punch, bobbing up and down with condiments and food, stretching around his counter to the farthest stools.

If he wasn't too busy, Jodi would let us read at his counter while we sipped our soft drinks or slurped the water melting from the last bits of ice. Among the hundreds of magazines and comic books in the liquor store, I had begun to take an interest in *Photography* and *True Confessions* ("I Was a Rich Man's Plaything"), which I read surreptitiously in the store, and I usually bought one or two comics, a Captain Marvel adventure (I liked the idea of a word transporting me wherever I wanted: "Shazam!") and a Walt Disney.

While not above insisting he was for little kids, I had enjoyed Walt Disney ever since my sister and I had taken the bus to Leeds to see *Fantasia*. On a cold, wet evening, we had waited in line at the cinema, only to have the ticket seller say that we were too young to see the film without an accompanying adult.

"Don't worry," June said to me, "we'll make our own parent."

She approached a kind-looking woman, explained our problem, and asked whether we might go into the cinema with her.

The woman dropped her cigarette, ground it with her foot, and said: "Stay with me, lovies. I'll see you get into this naughty film."

So now I bought the Donald Duck comics along with others like them. Yet I grew excited thinking of the magazines on the high shelves of the liquor store, already aware that they offered more

excitement than Walt Disney, excitement that neither Bungy nor Mrs. Brown nor my parents would
ever condone.

§

Besides the returned bottles, I had short-
lived sources of money from two of our neighbors.
Karl Ross was a German who lived directly across
the street, up the hill, that is, on the other side. He
had built around his house a kind of privacy wall,
which he wanted to extend in length and height.
He offered me one cent for every concrete block I
would carry up to the back of his garden. This was
harder work than gathering Coke bottles and less
lucrative. Still, through one hot day I struggled up
his steps, around the house, and up through the
garden, lugging the blocks. Except to frown occasionally and to bark what I guessed to be German,
Mr. Ross gave brief directions and otherwise ignored me. He didn't tell me I was working too
slowly, although I knew that he thought I was, and
he never said anything about stopping for a drink of
water or tea. When the Good Humor van came
round, driving enticingly by the house, Mr. Ross
ignored that too; I had hoped he might buy me a

1 2 9

popsicle or a chocolate vanilla stick to make me feel better. The Good Humor man saw no signal and drove down toward Jimmy Stewart's house where he always stopped. Normally a good worker (except in our own house), I hated this job and found an excuse not to return the next weekend. When, a few weeks later, I hit a ball through the front window of his house, I begged my father to speak with Mr. Ross. I confessed reluctantly to breaking the window, but I did not want to encounter that silent and stingy man.

Mrs. Silver was an old widow with thin white hair, who lived seven houses down the road. She had asked my grandmother whether one of those nice boys would like to go shopping for her and maybe do some chores. While I had heard the word *chores* from Jimmy Stewart, its meaning was new to me. Grandma explained, and I said I would like to try. On Saturday morning, I went to the little house, rang the doorbell, and was admitted into darkness. Each window was shaded by venetian blinds, through which only the faintest bars of light could enter. Mrs. Silver gave me her shopping list and sent me off with four dollars in my pocket. When I brought back the groceries, she asked me to do some work in the kitchen. I didn't mind the work, but the smell in the house overpowered me. Afraid of thieves, Mrs. Silver refused to open her windows. If someone came to the door, she looked through a telescopic spy hole to see who was there, then opened the door to allow as little intrusion as possible from the outside.

She asked me whether I had heard about the Israeli state, and the man who had become, she said, English like myself, and who was on his way to Israel to be the new president. I knew nothing of the people or events she mentioned, and it was a long time before I associated her pronunciation with Chaim Weizmann. Apparently I was not a good enough listener, or maybe the fifteen cents she paid me was too much money for this poor woman. In any case she did not ask me to come back. I was relieved not to enter that house again, but its smell clung to my nostrils long afterwards—a thoroughly sour smell, like milk so far gone that it had started to rot.

We met other neighbors in the first few weeks, and the Myers family in particular became our good friends. One day, digging up worms in the back-yard, I heard a terrible scream. A young girl was jumping up and down while trying to hold her badly bleeding foot. My sister and I both ran down the yard at the same time, and my sister, trained in first aid, wrapped a handkerchief around the girl's foot, squeezing it to try to stop the flow of blood. It was amazing how much poured out, even with the bandage. Then my mother came and brought a long scarf, which she used as a tourniquet (a word I didn't recognize at that time), twisting it around June's bandage until the bleeding stopped. The bottle that had sliced the girl's foot, and that I found soon after, had not cut tendons or done any lasting damage.

Later that evening, when her parents brought her back from the doctor, the girl was subdued and sobbed periodically, but she invited us down to watch their new television set. That marked the beginning of a new passion, a new era. To a boy fascinated by windows, this was for a long time my look into another world.

From the center of a "jumbo" Admiral console, the small, greenish tube threw bright pictures into darkness, flickering on pale faces. We watched Uncle Milty; Kukla, Fran, and Ollie; the Three Stooges movies; and the Bob Hope Show on KTLA.

Dick Lane kicked tires to indicate the high quality of cars at Felix Chevrolet. A tiny man with a loud voice called "for Philip Morreeees." I loved the talent shows, like Ed Sullivan's "Toast of the Town," with people performing several instruments, or singing what I came to know as country and western songs, or imitating the voices of movie stars. Sometimes we watched Howdy Doody Time, which we scorned without turning off. For my brother and me, the most engrossing programs remained professional wrestling, featuring Gorgeous George (who with his sequined robes and permed blond hair resembled Liberace without becoming any less a ferocious adversary), and the Roller Derby, which was orchestrated like a family fight, everybody intimate and angry with each other at the same time. Our star was Spider Webb with the L.A. T-Birds, who flung her elbows like wings to stagger opponents or whipped by the other team on the catapults of her teammates' arms.

My parents would have to telephone to pry us away from the Myers house, apologizing for our manners and truly not understanding why we preferred another house to our own. We did prefer the other house, where we felt welcome, where popcorn and ice-cream sandwiches, Cokes and hot chocolate, and other delicious things appeared frequently and in great amounts. While Jeannie and Mollie, the daughter who cut herself, seemed barely to tolerate us after a few months, their parents always managed to put us at ease. The fantasy of television and the warmth of the house made their living room preferable to our own, where— once my father had left for work—my mother stayed uncomfortable or unhappy with Grandma glaring from across the room. The two of them might sit all evening without speaking, Grandma sewing and Mother doing the crossword from the London *Times* or Manchester *Guardian*. Grandma had not told my parents that she intended to live in the house during the time they would be buying it from her.

The comfort of the Myers house suggested to me that Los Angeles held secrets behind other walls, as if a life might be found that still excluded me. On the way home from hours of television I would sometimes walk up and down our street, peering into windows of other houses, watching people eat or talk or play Ping-Pong or watch their televisions in the areas I could see. I knew that I shouldn't loiter in people's yards or intrude on their privacy, although I meant no harm. The light always seemed friendlier in those houses, the promise larger. I would dream of having another family, richer than these people maybe, but similarly happy, without sickness or poverty, where the food lay heaped on tables and the refrigerator offered endless choice. Brothers would be banned (some of the time) as well as grandmothers, and a private room in the house would be filled with my books and pictures of the Himalayas. My new parents would feel superior; they would talk easy American talk, and I would share their fluency. I might even outtalk Jimmy Stewart.

❧

Occasionally we would watch the real Jimmy Stewart (in films like *Destry*) at the Glassell Park movie house, about a mile away from where we lived. If my father was able to begin work late or if my mother felt well enough to be left off with us, we would go down as much for the bingo show, which took place between the double feature, as for the movies themselves. The owner or manager of the movie house would call out numbers for cards we received with our tickets, walking back and forth on the apron of the stage yelling "Ni-en," "Ze-ro," "BINGO!" Bingo might be worth "a buck" or "ten bucks," and though we never won, I thought of winning as another possible way to our new life.

᳓

In the eight years since the 1940 census, Los Angeles has absorbed a population roughly equal to that of Cincinnati's (455,610). It now claims a population of 1,904,725. It has passed Detroit and is pressing close to Philadelphia. Every month about 10,000 more people move in to stay. . . . It now ranks first in four industries: aircraft, motion pictures, oil-well equipment, sportswear manufacture. . . . For 61-year-old Mayor Bowron, a chronic worrier, this has merely meant more problems to worry about, e.g., how to get more houses, more schools, more water, more express highways. Says he of his city's increasing bigness: "I hated to see it come, but here it is."

Time, 1948

It was odd to read this kind of report, as we did read them, daily in the *Los Angeles Times* or in *Time* and *Life,* the usual magazines (along with *Reader's Digest* and *National Geographic*) in my grandmother's house.

"We are like so many exiled numbers," my mother said, "seeking a place in the statistics."

We learned that Mr. Ross was an immigrant, but so too was Mr. Andersen, the man next door with the purple birthmark on his face, who came from Sweden; and Naomi Allen, the English woman up the road, who had set a world record in glider flying; and Manuel Duarte, who worked for Uncle George, and who was born in Mexico; and others who weren't so obvious, or who came from unspellable places like Massachusetts and Connecticut.

Within a week or so of arriving, we had to go with my parents in Uncle George's car to see Aunt Vinnie, who had emigrated from England and had lived at first in Lawrence, Massachusetts, where she and her husband worked in a great mill. They were skilled dyers, lured to the United States from Yorkshire, who had then decided to follow friends from the East Coast to Southern California. Aunt Vinnie was a tiny woman whose clothes and house—she lived alone now—came out of another era. She told us that the house had been built in four working days, along with similar houses in the neighborhood. All were stuccoed cottages from the 1920s, with two-track concrete driveways leading to single garages at the rear of the lots. Aunt Vinnie was proud of her 1932 Model A roadster, which sat, covered by a blanket, in the garage. It was years, she said, since anyone had driven the car, yet she cared too much to give it up. She let my brother and me sit behind the wheel and adjust the hand accelerator, pretending to drive and smelling the mixed odors of old gasoline and decayed upholstery. We wondered if she might give us the car, at least in another six years when I could drive.

Aunt Vinnie's house was shadowed by new buildings across from her property, commercial buildings and large apartment houses that dwarfed her house and kept her living room in a twilight gloom. Aunt Vinnie still sat in a rocker on her front porch, as if she could look across open spaces to the foothills or down in the direction of Los Angeles.

She cried when she said goodbye to my mother, and I remember her waving at us as we drove away, shouting "Come again, come again, come again." That was the only time I saw her.

§

Because my father and uncle worked mostly at night, though sometimes from late afternoon to eight or nine in the morning, we could occasionally take sightseeing trips during the day. One day Uncle George decided we needed to see the Pacific Ocean at Malibu or Zuma, where it remained, he said, untamed and unspoiled. On the way, he described the mating habits of the grunion, a trout-sized fish which had been seen as far away as the Japan Sea, but which came to Southern California beaches to lay its eggs. The female fish would wiggle herself into the sand, while the male would wrap himself around her and fertilize the eggs. This happened, however, only at full moon and on certain beaches. He said that he had often been at the beaches when the grunion were running. One could pick them up from the sand and cook them on the spot. Nothing tasted better. Still, he said, he felt guilty, because grunion were an emblem of California, getting there at all costs, giving up their lives in the struggle. He spoke of John Steinbeck's novel *The Grapes of Wrath,* and I heard for the first time about dust bowls that drove people here to California from other parts of the United States. I wondered about what Uncle George said and whether we ourselves were a kind of grunion, special and common at the same time, five out of the ten thousand people arriving in California that month. How could ten thousand of us all find places to live? Would there be space enough—and food? Maybe Mrs. Brown was right.

I was to see no grunion for years to come. That day we drove up Verdugo Road, through Glendale, which Uncle Bill had told us was "all white," to the San Fernando Valley, which we knew from the song: "I'll make the San Fernando Valley my home." We went first to Chatsworth because George wanted us to see the setting of so many westerns, films that he himself would not go to see—just as he had never before seen Chatsworth. And it did occur to my brother and me that we recognized shapes of rock and stretches of wild, rough land, an uncanny copy of itself in film, where cowboys fought in dance halls for gold and justice and beautiful heroines.

After driving south again, we turned up into foothills and along Topanga Canyon, from the top of which we could look back down the valley to Los Angeles and ahead to the ocean. "When, like stout Cortez," my mother said, "we stared at the Pacific." We ate foot-long hot dogs from the back of a catering truck, spooning on green relish and ketchup. Mother settled for a tea bag dipped in tepid water and smiled with amusement as we ate.

Announcing that it was time for a snapshot, my father fetched the new Brownie that Grandma had lent us, a tiny, plastic camera that focused itself and took small, grainy photographs, to be sent to Grandma Woodhouse and other relatives in Yorkshire. Forty years later my brother and I are still laughing and poking each other in the faded image. My sister sits formally, pretending her brothers don't exist, while my mother shades her eyes in her habitual way, staring beyond us into a world of her own. I imagine my father behind the camera, making a silly pun about brown pictures or Mr. Brown or brownouts—if they used the word then— squeezing the little button that captures a moment as if it had a meaning or special quality waiting to be discovered, or as if "Topanga, November 1948" said all that needed to be said.

George, who avoided photographs, called us to the car for the drive down to the coast. He was right. Except for straggling kelp or occasional out-croppings of rock, Malibu had almost perfect sand. Waves rose smoothly to shatter on distant headlands or on the edge of the beach. The water was cold, but we swam and played for much of the afternoon in the sunshine, and after our picnic June and I rented large paddleboards that took us lightly out across the waves. I soon learned that while June, who was a strong swimmer, could paddle back against the undertow, I could not. However hard I flailed with my arms, I moved farther and farther from shore, the paddleboard aimed fixedly toward Japan.

I thought of last year's school trip to Northern Ireland, and Belfast Lough. Three of us who were all nonswimmers had rented a large rowboat and rowed out into choppy waters, far from shore, where we could no longer control the oars. Secretly relieved to know we would be rescued, we pre-tended at first not to hear or see Bungy when he drew near, screaming and waving in the prow of another rowboat, to tow us back to the dock. Now when I managed to peer back to the shore, no one seemed to be worried, and I could not bring myself to cry out, because I was at least as ashamed as I was scared. I counted seconds until sharks would eat me—one and two and three and four and—or tried to estimate how long it would be before I was wholly out of sight. Then slowly the paddleboard swung round and the coast began to move back again forgivingly. I could see my sister, following me down the edge of the water.

When at last I returned to shore she was waiting, about a mile down the beach, and we had to leave the paddleboard in order to fetch my father to help us carry it. I played out of the water after that, settling for sand castles and races down the beach with my brother.

We drove home by a different route, first along the coast, with the ocean turning silver gold in the late afternoon sun. At Santa Monica my uncle pointed inland and said:

"Thomas Mann, the novelist, lives up there; he's just published a new book." My parents apparently didn't recognize the name. "He got out of Germany under Hitler, lived in Switzerland, and came here. His new book's about Faust and music, in other words about Germany. Odd to have written it in Santa Monica. But you know," my uncle continued, "lots of writers have come to this area, even Englishmen like Huxley. He lives in Hollywood. And then there's Evelyn Waugh, who has my undying gratitude for savaging Forest Lawn. You haven't read *The Loved One*? It almost makes you feel privileged to be in such a topsy-turvy world."

"Did you hear about those Estonians, or were they Latvians, who arrived in the States last month? Came in a boat smaller than the *Mayflower* all the way from Sweden. They thought the Russians might still be after them. And speaking of Russians, what about Gorbals, the Glasgow slum? The Commies lost that one too, last month, when Labor won again. I wonder how many of those people would like to come to California—especially on a day like this. Waugh caught only the crazy part of California. What I'm suggesting, Lorna, is that you don't have it so bad."

"George," my father said, when my mother didn't reply. "You know nothing about the Glasgow poor, still less about your sister-in-law. Let's get back."

Now we drove away from the coast, up Santa Monica Boulevard for our first glimpse of Beverly Hills and Hollywood, and stopped at a drive-in restaurant for a malted milk.

"No, don't get out," said Uncle George. "They serve us in the car." We squirmed on the warm seats, burning from sand and salt, while a waitress in tight shorts roller-skated to take our order, then to bring it on trays that hung like little scaffolds on the windows and the outside of the doors.

That night I shivered from sunburn, remembering cold malts on burning lips, my back paper-tight and tingling, and I went to sleep paddling through deep waters to watch the grunion mating on moonlit sands.

❦

I had never been so cold. All the way from Giggleswick we had been treading in snow, which was loose and blowing, obscuring the path as we plodded uphill. My footsteps would not reach my father's, so I made two to his one, and every few steps Dave gave me a push from behind. I wore a thick one-piece "siren" suit—usually the best protection against cold—which today was not helping. The white was frightening: white fields, or what we could see of them, and white clothes as the snow stuck more and more. By contrast the limestone walls looked almost gray, except where the wind had rammed the snow into holes and crevices. Snowflakes stung my eyes like thistles or glued, freezing, to my face.

At last it got so cold that I called to my father, who looked ahead and around and nodded, as if he too were glad to stop. Almost immediately and directly in front of us we found a tunnel, no more than a yard wide, cut deep into the limestone cliff. Inside, my father rubbed gently my chilblained feet and hands, and Dave winked and divided a Cadbury bar from his pack. I dreaded going on, and when my father suggested giving up and returning to Skipton, I felt warm and joyous for the first time all day. For a while we sat and ate our frozen sandwiches and looked out at the blizzard, which seemed so safely framed by the cave's entrance. Then we almost tripped down the mountain, sliding and laughing, making fun of the snow and ourselves. Later we drank scalding milky coffee in a coffee bar in Skipton Square. I felt like Scott or Mallory, content with defeat that had become an accomplishment. Although we had turned back in snow and wind, tomorrow we would make our best attempt. That is what Mallory would have said when resisted by Everest. But tomorrow I was eating roast beef for Sunday dinner, and trying to eat Brussels sprouts, in the steamy kitchen at home. Langcliffe Scar was far away and far behind. Outside it was raining.

We had begged my father to take us up Eaton Canyon, so that we could climb the old coach road to Mount Wilson, which Jimmy Stewart said was the best hike in the San Gabriel Mountains. One day, my father persuaded George to drive us to Altadena and to meet us a few hours later on top of the mountain. My mother stayed at home because of pain in her legs, but the rest of the family set off, climbed up the stony foothills, and found the stream that flowed through ragged and secluded rocky canyons, each more enclosed and satisfying than the one below. The sun was as hot as midsummer sun, bleaching the land and drawing out odors

1 4 7

of oils and sap, of tiny flowers, sage, and scrubby chaparral. Stones felt hot to the touch. Lizards eyed us from shady places and refused to move. Above, instead of curlews, hawks were circling, drawing patterns in the oversize sky. When we had rinsed in one of the cold, clear ponds, we ate our sandwiches and fruit and drank tea from our school thermos bottles. Afterwards we scrambled across to the coach road, a gravel track zigzagging up steep slopes, every turn giving another look back at the distant flatlands. In time the brush country gave way to small pines, then larger pines, until the air became a hot breath of pine tar and needles, and we lay, tired and sweating, in the shadows of the tall trees.

At last we stood on top of Mount Wilson among the observatory buildings, saw the great telescope, and squinted through coin-operated binocular tele-scopes down the slopes we had climbed. The entire way up we had seen nobody. Now we were among crowds and traffic jams on the mountain peak, as if the city had driven to meet us. It didn't seem right that people could drive up a mountain, where they threw candy wrappers and bottles on the roadside and enjoyed the view without the work. Even though George was driving a car, I was glad when he arrived to take us away.

"The truth is," George was saying, "Americans even make pilgrimages by car, whether going to church, going to shop, going to Mount Wilson. Personally, I'm a true Angeleno. I love cars. I admit they are merely machines to do a job and that luxury and size and aesthetics should be unimportant. Maybe I'm a sucker for clever advertising—or bad puns. Packards 'designed by the Wizard of Ah's.' But I think, Jerry, that America somehow *is* the car: one great big Detroit. I can tell you about Packard's straight-eight engines, about the design of the Studebaker, about the brakes on the new Nash, about the 'Air Foam' seats in this car, which seem to me more comfortable than anything in our house. Believe it or not, I sometimes go and sit in my car in the evening. Also no doubt to get away from Minnie."

My father told about his little Austin, which lacked a working starter motor and which Mother had to push each morning before the engine would turn over. That had been long before the war. It was painful, he said, on the coldest mornings, when he had to drive with his head out of the window, the ice refusing to melt from the windscreen.

"That's wind*shield*. American words for American things. When you get your car, I recommend one of the new Fords or a used Hudson, like mine. This has a cork clutch, which accounts for the smooth shift, and it is a very strong, sure automobile."

My father said he wondered how any "automobile" could be altogether sure when speeding round mountain curves, but my uncle didn't seem to listen. He was telling us about the end of rail transportation in Los Angeles and how Firestone and General Motors and probably the oil companies were dismantling the Pacific Electric system, considered, he said, to have been the best in the country.

"And to be honest, I don't really care. Cars mean a lot to me, streetcars don't. It's not just technology or privacy, either," he said. "You know, when I was in college—and I graduated summa cum laude, which I tell you for the story, not to boast—my asthma was so bad that I couldn't do the ordinary things with other students. No one spent more time in the library, and for me it was a simple necessity. On hot or muggy days I'd have to sit on the side of the road waiting for my breath to come back, wondering whether I could reach home. Father died of asthma, and I was afraid I might, too. So a car for me is health and freedom, and a good car is more health and freedom. Do you see what I mean? We'll ignore the irony that I went into a line of work lethal for an elephant, let alone an asthmatic." He stopped talking, coughed, and said:

"Can you imagine anyone with breathing problems starting an office maintenance service? It's like father with *his* asthma moving to Seattle, which, of course, he did. Well, I suppose I've got used to it. And you will, too. June, Carl, Paul: would you like an ice cream? There's a Wright's ice-cream parlor just down the road."

(Was that the evening we went to a drive-in movie somewhere near Hollywood? Our car like a hundred others is attached to a post and points in homage to the distant screen, where Vincent Price

1 5 1

as the Baron of Arizona mouths words somehow un-
connected with the sound box hanging in the car.
"I've known many women, but with you . . . I'm
afraid." My sister giggles and reminds me of Dirty
Gertie Bannister, who carried round a tray of tea
cakes during the intermission at Rodley Cinema
and made tea on a portable gas ring. "With her,"
June says, "I'm afraid.")

§

George was what my father called a night
person, someone who preferred his own company to
that of other people, but also someone who could
only sleep during the day. Office maintenance allowed him the kind of quiet that he loved. Sometimes he would stop work and read, just as he might
stop conversation, in a restaurant, for example, by
pulling out a book. In another sense, he was not
alone at night. He listened much of the time to his
radio, which he took carefully from one job to another, unwinding the wire antenna and tuning in to
a program that solicited audience phone calls. He
would call from time to time with a piece of information or a plea for Esperanto, or would work,
chuckling, as he listened to others, with many of

whose voices he became familiar. For all his avoidance of people, he would attend an annual picnic sponsored by the radio station, so that he could put a face to the voices he had heard. I wondered if the other people associated George's husky, deep voice with the crew-cutted, word-filled man who had become my uncle.

⁊

Not long after our arrival my father met Ben and Madge Young, a childless couple from Yorkshire, from the Windhill area of Shipley, not far from our own village or from the Brontë country nearby. Although quite unwell, my mother insisted on inviting them to dinner, and dinner by that time was already predictable. She placed a large and bony piece of beef—still calling it a "joint"—in the oven at ten in the morning, cooking it until it was tender but also tasteless. She bought Van de Kamp's bread from Robert's, along with Brussels sprouts, potatoes—to make mashed potatoes—and vanilla ice cream. (Later she would substitute chicken for beef, the other ingredients remaining the same, except that the potatoes became instant mashed and a frozen apple pie complemented the ice cream.) It was as though she woke up one day hating food and hating still more its preparation. At the same time, she took pleasure in serving people, if at all possible, and would often try to cook when she should have rested—or when my sister, with less effort, could have made a better meal.

The Youngs, gentle people who seemed permanently lost, spoke respectfully about "Southern California," as if it were a holy shrine they had reached, its mysteries still to be discovered. They were delighted to find sympathetic people from Yorkshire, and Ben told us about the English colony in Los Angeles, with its cricket and bowling and what he thought its snobbish institutions. He admitted to feeling awkward among most of his countrymen, possibly thinking that his dialect worked against him here as it had at home. Through most of the dinner Madge did the talking, my parents and Ben nodding or interjecting a few remarks. After finishing his food, Ben began to talk. He was, he said, faced with a real setback.

An accountant by training, he had taken a job in Southern California divorced from everything he knew.

"It's a plastics factory, see, and I have to tell

you, Lorna, the smell is something awful. No fresh air from the time you enter that door until the time you leave—and we punch a clock, as they say, with a card in a little clock-machine. When I landed a job there I was much relieved. It was work and it put food on the table. I'm a chap who likes to be useful, to do my bit. My responsibility is molding a small plastic cylinder, open at one end, closed except for a tiny hole at the other. My coworkers told me we were making something for national defense, which sounded important enough. Well, I never! I've just discovered what I really do."

He reached into his pocket and brought out half a dozen of the items, each in a different color.

"Take a peek," he said. When I looked into the tiny hole, I could see a smiling woman in a bathing suit, waving in my direction. I didn't understand at first, but it turned out that Ben had been making a kind of key chain to be handed out by car dealers. He was mortified, he said, but he laughed when my parents laughed and leaned over and kissed his wife.

"What a place, Jerry. What a place, Lorna. But you know, we're going to stay. I won't make peep shows all my life."

My parents often joked about Ben Young, yet they continued to see him, as they did a number of people who happened to come from England. My mother was especially fond of Naomi Allen, who spoke so elegantly and who, instead of flying airplanes as she had during the war (and before when she set her records), now lived with a real estate agent and "handled properties." Her mother was "titled," my mother said, living comfortably in the south of England where they might someday visit her. Naomi prided herself on avoiding organizations like the Yorkshire Club and scoffed at people who got together for no reason except that they were born in a certain region. Nonetheless, she must have sought out my parents as they sought out her because they shared some notion of a common past. My mother even started to take an interest in English royalty (as well as teacups) within a few weeks of our arrival in Los Angeles. In England she had scorned the royal family, saying that she wouldn't go to the bottom of the Rodley Lane to see one of them. Now she followed news accounts about the birth of a prince, later named Charles, along with the failing health of King George. She also kept silent about Winston Churchill, who—after Hitler—had been the arch-villain at home. It was hard to fault Churchill among people who revered him as the national British hero or thought of his politics as necessary medicine for an ailing England.

But beyond this, I think my parents shifted in their own values. They did not praise Attlee much any more; they developed some reservations about the nationalizing of the railways; and they had expanded their sense of things British, so that former enemies or things despised slowly became tolerable, even valuable, in retrospect. For my mother the shift in values meant that she began to recall England in ways she had never known it and in ways, too, that assumed no future change. While I read articles in *National Geographic* about "Seeking Mindanao's Strangest Creatures" or "My Life in the Valley of the Moon" (as well as those that showed half-naked women in Africa and the South Pacific), my mother read "The Curlew's Secret" and "By Cotswold Lanes to Wold's End." When she spoke of going home, even my brother and I recognized that she wanted to go back to a place existing only in her loneliness.

My father kept most of his feelings to himself, unless my mother's health or debilitating fatigue broke down his reserves, and he pleaded with us as if we were equals or, which was worse, could do something to help.

"Let's try to make your mother happy," he might say, and my brother and sister would look, as I'm sure I looked, baffled by the appeal. What could make her happy? More cigarettes or tea? More quiet? If by not fighting we could make a difference, we would promise not to fight, until the struggle not to fight led us, almost inevitably, to another loud and futile exchange.

🍃 One Friday afternoon, my father looked especially worn.

"Carl, would you like to go to work with me tonight?"

By this time, he had bought his own 1947 Hudson, a twin for my uncle's, and I would have accepted any invitation to drive with him. I can still remember each of the buildings we went to that evening, and what I did to help. While my father swept, with green sawdustlike sweeping compound, or mopped with an impregnated dust mop, I emptied the wastepaper baskets and washed the glass tops of the desks with paper towels. I showed so much reluctance to clean toilets that my father did that, although I forced myself to wipe out the ashtrays, which were full of cigar and cigarette butts or coated with a foul-smelling syrup that took my breath away. It was as if all the air had been sucked out of these buildings, leaving only stale, dusty emptiness.

"As George would say, you get used to it. Still, it is pretty awful. You develop an altogether different perspective on human life, and I don't mean simply that all people look the same at their stool. Odd, but it seems that I've been at this now for years instead of weeks. The worst of it may be that I *am* getting used to it."

We went first to a place called Los Angeles Brick and Tile, a relatively clean building, with reddish tile floors, then on to perhaps the dirtiest place I had ever seen, two grimy offices of the Los Angeles Boiler Works. Out near the warehouse stood rust-red drums and steel boilers, some of them a story high. The offices, almost too small for both of us to move around in, were a uniform beige color, from the walls to the porcelain of the toilet. I remember that it took exactly twenty minutes for us to clean the rough linoleum floors and dust the furniture, twirling the feather dusters like wands.

Since we were making what my father called "good time," we were able to stop for a cup of tea and a piece of pie in a diner. We went on next to a large plant somewhere east of downtown. This was where we had our problems. As we lifted the cleaning equipment out of the trunk of the Hudson, which already smelled of chemicals, a van pulled up behind us. Three oversize men, two of them black men, emerged slowly, scowled at my father and the broom and feather duster in his hand, while slouching toward us.

"Stay where you are, sonny," the white man said. I stayed where I was, too frightened to move, yet fully aware that my brother would have rushed at the men and attacked them, long before he could say what was happening, and even if he knew he had no chance.

"Hold it there, scab. Let me guess. You're an honorary member of the union?"

It was obvious that my father had no idea what

they meant. I'm sure he was frightened, too, but he smiled at the man who asked and said:

"I'm sorry, sir, but I don't know which union you mean."

"Our union, motherfuck. Janitors' union."

Gradually the three men had closed in on my father and were pushing him against the wall of the building. I noticed how slight he was, how short he seemed next to these men.

"Where's your union card?"

One of the men hit my father, not hard, with his open hand, telling him they didn't have all night. My father somehow kept his poise and explained to them that he didn't know about a union but would gladly join if necessary and if they would give him the information. Suddenly a lot less threatening, they backed away from him, describing how and when he had to join. Without membership, they said, he would not be so lucky next time, and it might not be smart to bring his kid along. Then they climbed back in the van and drove off.

My father stood there for a few seconds breathing hard, his face clown-white under the lamps.

"That's George for you," he said at last. "He's never mentioned a union to me, just leaves me to be attacked by ruffians."

Ruffians already sounded odd to my ears, and I laughed, partly from relief, partly because my father sounded so out of place. He laughed, too, and we went in and cleaned the new building, joking about ruffians and knocking teeth out and fighting union pressures and freeing workers to clean filthy offices. Later, nevertheless, my father was obliged to join the union, at a cost he could not easily afford.

"I don't mind belonging to a union," he would say. "I've always felt that the worst jobs should be the best paid. Coal miners for a start. It's the principle that bothers me, the intimidation, the lack of choice. Then again, I suppose I've given up a great deal of choice in the past few months."

🦢

We awoke one morning to hear screams from my parents' bedroom. My brother and I must have opened our eyes at the same time and were staring at each other, forgetting last night's fight.

1 6 2

"It's Mom," he said, jumping out of bed and running down the hall. I followed more slowly, in time to see Grandma stop him at the door and say that Mother had been sick, that the doctor was with her and she should be fine soon.

"But what's wrong?" Paul asked, his own voice competing with renewed cries from inside the room.

"Your mother is very upset. The doctor'll give her a pill. Don't worry."

After a few minutes my father came out of the room. He was still wearing a dressing gown and was unshaven and gray in his face, but he tried to smile at Paul. He didn't see me because I was farther away, afraid to approach that room.

"She's quiet now," he said. "Just get dressed and have breakfast. The more quiet the better." Without explaining, he acted as if we understood. And maybe Paul did. Even though he was a year and a half younger, he always seemed older when he needed to be.

"Come on," he said. "We have to be out of the house."

I never did see the doctor, but later in the

morning an ambulance arrived and took my mother to the hospital. They must have put her to sleep, for she lolled on the stretcher and evidently didn't see us. Father got into the ambulance with her, urging us not to worry and asking June to make dinner. Then the ambulance drove away, and the three of us, looking at each other and up the steps at Grandma, stood without speaking for a few seconds more. Grandma looked back down at us, shaking her head, and she went inside and closed the door.

"I'm going to run away," I said.

"Just run down to the market first," my sister said. "We need food for dinner."

That was the first of Mother's trips to the hospital. Since we weren't allowed to visit her, we didn't know which hospital or hospitals she went to or what they did. Once I heard Grandma and Uncle George talking about electroshock, which I read about in a magazine, and I always expected my mother to come home without memory, without knowing who I was. How could you then convince her that you were her son? How could you remember for her? How explain?

"Daddy," I said, "what does 'Murika Mure' mean?"

We were standing on a bleak hill near Morley, gazing across at smokestacks and clusters of attached houses, patchy at first before merging in the distance with the rooftops and chimneys of Leeds. My father laughed, apologized, and laughed louder.

"You don't understand Mrs. Hunter. She means 'America Moor.' And this is it. Let's hope the real America looks more promising."

My father, Paul, and I had just returned from a week in the Lake District, where we had gone after emptying the house in Brookfield. We were to stay with a friend of Aunt Edith, a Mrs. Hunter, who had two extra rooms, and who had recommended that we take an afternoon walk on "Murika Mure." We were waiting for the train to bring back Mother and June from their cycling trip through Somerset and Devon. I had wanted to go with them, having seen the railway posters of Devon—graceful, pastel villages, set on the edge of a light green sea, with a church spire and flowers, and miniature people playing on the sands. "GWR. Paddington Station. 1s." For some reason, my father had chosen to go north, while my mother went south. Only after all these years do I wonder why we didn't travel together. The three of us hiked on Helvellyn and Skiddaw, stayed at Grasmere and Kendal, walked around Thirlmere, which served, my father told us, as the water supply for Manchester. It disturbed me that this peaceful lake should have to travel to a noisy, distant city.

I don't know what went wrong with that trip, but it rained every day, with mist hanging off the crags, farmhouses shut up as if for winter, and the roads empty of people. The youth hostels themselves, normally full and noisy, were desolate, and I felt like an unwelcome guest wherever we decided to spend the night. It was a relief to take the bus to Ambleside and to catch the train back to Leeds.

But as it turned out, Morley offered no improvement. A cold wind was blowing, with fine drops of rain, which stung the face and numbed it at the same time. My father pointed toward Gipton, where Grandma Dawson lived, and the area where, he said, we could see Lucas Street, such as it was. I knew that my parents and June had lived in Grandma Dawson's house on Lucas Street when my father had been unemployed. June had described

166

going to the outhouse, which was down the street and quite far from the house. She said that she refused, as a girl of two, to use the rank toilet and had to be admitted to the Leeds Infirmary. Disheartened by the conditions, Mother had moved out, back to her parents' house, taking June with her. All this I knew without my father saying anything else. And I felt somehow that he was thinking of that time, too. We stood there, wet and cold, until he unbelted his raincoat, looked at us sideways, and started to run.

"Last one back to Mrs. Hunter's pays for the *Queen Elizabeth*." He always ran faster than we did, so we could only follow, laughing and stumbling and tripping each other back to afternoon tea.

Early the next morning we took the train to London.

༄

5

I give you back 1948.
I give you all the years from then
to the coming one. Give me back the moon
with its frail light falling across a face.
                    Philip Levine, "You Can Have It"

What occurs to me now is how I *might* have told this story, or—for whatever reasons—how unimportant a story as such has come to seem. I think of alternatives:

In the fall of 1948, my parents left England for a new life in Los Angeles. This is an account, or rather no account but a series of impressions, about the journey and the circumstances surrounding the journey. As our minds did at the time, I move back and forth between the Old World and the New, one part of the journey and another. Two facts are of some importance: first, my father's family by a quirk of history already lived in Los Angeles; second, my mother's bad health and the generally depressed conditions in Yorkshire persuaded my parents to make the change. My mother never recovered from her uprooting; my father suffered through difficult times. Occasionally I have followed my father's and mother's memories as if they were my own, which in a sense they have become.

This may not be radically different from what I have imagined, except that it gives the speaker a kind of authority I have not sought while seeking to justify what I have tried to write. Another telling might call for a definite beginning:

In the fall of 1947 my parents told us that we would be moving to Los Angeles. . . .

Or:

We left Leeds Central Station at six o'clock in the morning. . . .

But perhaps after all there are no beginnings to stories such as this, and no clear ends. Thinking about beginnings is itself a way of coming to terms with the end of what I have written, which is a kind of spiral or continued re-turning to a past that has become obsessive. It would not be true to say that I had to write about November 1948. No one has to write. It is true that the people, the spaces, the smells of that time have come back in powerful and recurrent images, as if seeking to be written, as if Mnemosyne, mother of the Muses, has been quietly insistent.

Philip Levine's poem about giving back 1948 comes to mind again, and with it the faces that have through the years slipped out of the light. It is ten years since my mother died, ten years to the week as I write this sentence; and it is forty years since my family took that train to London, then the boat train and the *Queen Elizabeth* and the other trains to Los Angeles. It is also seventy years since that first memory, which was my mother's and is now mine, of her skipping visit to my grandfather as he guarded the iron railway bridge at the time of Passchendaele, or any other of those meaningless battles with the beautiful names, during the Great War.

At times that kind of dating matters, as if to frame a life or to touch patterns and events beyond our own by placing ourselves in history. And I have thought about that ten-year-old boy living at the time of the Berlin airlift, or the fall (it was always the fall) of China to the Communist forces, or the scrapping of the Bikini fleet, hopelessly contaminated by the new hydrogen bomb. Where lies the crossing of an individual life with public events, and do we hold on to those events because they are the real stuff of history, whatever that might mean, or because they offer milestones useful for ourselves?

For when we look back to our early years it is as passionate historians. What we see may be undramatic and unwilled, directed by an inner and self-selecting camera. The actual distance in time doesn't matter. What matters is the intensity, the unaccountable intensity of a particular era in our lives, around which (to change the metaphor) we piece together those remnants of recollected and imagined events that make us who we think we are. We live, as the Irish novelist and autobiographer George Moore wrote, in and for our memories, which are always our present as well as our past. If I tell friends or family (or, in moments of weakness, total strangers) about my own past, I mention such details as the fruit being hurled from the stern of the *Queen Elizabeth* or the announcement that

Harry Truman had won the election (or, rather, that Dewey had lost it) or the fact that my father went out to live with family he had either never seen or not seen for thirty-five years. I tell of my Los Angeles, which—disregarding the almost daily headlines about the new "smog"—remains clear-skied, shimmering in the morning light, a place of hope and sadness, beginning and end: our new beginning, the start of my mother's long unhappiness.

While knowing that I cannot reenter the mind of the child I was, any more than I can know the person who, apparently, grew out of the child, I have tried to honor memory, to give back that time forty years ago, witnessing again the events, the people, above all the impressions. Still, memories are at once more and less than things remembered. When I "look back" to see my father standing on America Moor, "looking ahead" to his journey, to the new life for his children, or perhaps, in a self-deluding moment, to new health for his wife, I think I see him, but, of course, I also see myself, placed by memory in a scene once witnessed and that could not have included me as viewer. In the words that the Queen uses to Alice, I have been "living backwards," memory working—as the Queen says—both ways, by which I mean a return to the time of my family's journey and a coming to terms with its effects, a forward remembering, one consequence of which is the need to write this memoir.

To write about oneself at an early age is to re-imagine rather than simply reconstruct, and we re-imagine a past from an odd ragbag of memories, all of which are pieces, some of which seem not to belong, along with others which ought to have happened, let us say, even if they did not. Beginning with glimpses, we soon tell stories. The past is neither chronological nor meaningful, except in our fictions, which are at once the memories themselves and our versions of them in whatever words we have struggled with to bring them forth.

Language, as the poet Milosz has said, may be our only homeland; I think of it more as a sign of exile. And writing, which is language unvoiced or translated, points to the same paradox. If it begins with a longing for homeland, it ends by telling our exile—inescapably so in a story about uprooting and change. A stranger might not care about my struggles with language, but possibly we all care about selves re-created from the shambles of the past, about lost homelands and shared exile.

Or is it more than this? Do we share our pasts in ways that are not so much collective as parallel or overlapping, at the same time barred from each other except through the scattered images, the sounds, the smells, the visions, that are exclusively, ineradicably our own? My memory of train sounds—goods or freight trains, high-speed expresses—howling through the Yorkshire night are mine, because I heard them long ago in that distant second-floor room and because I imagined as I listened the places from which the trains came and the places, too, to which they were going, whether London or Edinburgh, Bristol or Birmingham. Yet those sounds are bits of a larger music we all hear, however deaf at times, when one note or one bar suggests to us an entire, lost rhythm—and all the laughter and the sorrow that come with it.

I am sad to think of how much that matters has been left out or has taken its own, independent course, censoring as well as imagining. I know, for example, that I have done little justice to some of my family, because feelings of that time still focus my remembering. Where is my mother who could walk and run and laugh with the rest of us?

> *Music of bird, shepherd and rill*
> *Fill the air, as they always will;*
> *Always will, if you but stay*
> *To really listen to what they say. . . .*

I do listen and hear a soft laughter or perhaps a whistle in imitation of summer birds or the sounds of her voice recalling her own verses. I see her, feet dangling over a wall, merry with June, Paul, and me, her fingers touching my father's neck. We are on holiday near Dacre Bank, in the Yorkshire Dales. The photograph shows high, full cheeks, short hair cropped a little below the ears, a blouse open at the neck. All of us are swinging our feet, and we seem at once aware of the camera, to which we turn, and quite unself-conscious, as if we have just seen another rabbit scurry down a hole or have picked up trout for tonight's feast.

Without having touched this photograph in many years, I see it before me, a split second in one family's life, and I can, as memory invites, redevelop it in my thoughts and relive what may or may not have been. Yet how far away I am from the figures sitting on that wall almost half a century ago. How faintly words can give them back.